PRAISE FOR *BAKE IT 'TIL YOU MAKE IT*

"Molly is an inspiration and a breath of fresh air! Her faith, passion, and drive are infectious, and reading this book is like having a conversation with your coolest aunt!"

–Brian Duffy, Chef, TV Personality, and Hospitality Consultant

"Molly Bz proves that success isn't luck; it's discipline, faith, and consistent action. This book will challenge you to rise. She turns vision into action in *Bake It 'Til You Make It*. If you're ready to stop playing small, this is your next read."

–Real Talk Kim, Pastor, Limitless Church, and Author

"Molly didn't follow a recipe—she rewrote the rules of the category and built something the industry didn't see coming."

–Richard Montanez, former Vice President, PepsiCo, and Innovator, Flamin' Hot line of products including Hot Cheetos

"This book is so refreshing, written just the way Molly lives her life. Down to earth and recognizing God at every turn. Molly, what a powerful woman of God you are—God has exciting roads ahead and I will be praying for you. Blessings."

—Mayor Edna DeVries, Mayor of the Matanuska-Susitna Borough, Palmer, Alaska

BAKE IT
'TIL YOU
MAKE IT

ALSO BY MOLLY BLAKELEY

How to Be Fearless in Business

BAKE IT 'TIL YOU MAKE IT

The Story of a Risk-Taking Cookie Queen

MOLLY BLAKELEY

MATT HOLT

Matt Holt Books

An Imprint of BenBella Books, Inc.

Dallas, TX

The events, locations, and conversations in this book, while true, are recreated from the author's memory. However, the essence of the story and the feelings and emotions evoked are intended to be accurate representations. In certain instances, names, persons, organizations, and places have been changed to protect an individual's privacy.

MATT HOLT
BENBELLA

Matt Holt is an imprint of BenBella Books, Inc.
BenBella Books, Inc.
8080 N. Central Expressway
Suite 1700
Dallas, TX 75206
benbellabooks.com
Send feedback to feedback@benbellabooks.com

Matt Holt and *BenBella* are federally registered trademarks.

Printed in the United States of America
10 9 8 7 6 5 4 3 2 1

Library of Congress Control Number: 2026021458
ISBN 9798902680086 (hardcover)
ISBN 9798902680093 (electronic)

Editing by Katie Dickman
Copyediting by Michael Fedison
Proofreading by Jenny Bridges and Sarah Vostok
Text design and composition by Aaron Edmiston
Cover design by Morgan Carr
Cover photo by Jon Taylor; image © Adobe Stock / starlineart
Printed by Lake Book Manufacturing

This book is dedicated to my family: my husband, Aaron; Emerald, Anni, Luke; my grandson, Henry; son-in-law, Aaron; my brothers Tony, Jay, Sam, Sean, Jesse; my parents, Norm and Barb Blakeley, and my late mother, Sally Hoskins; and my brothers Andy, Jason, and Leland. For their love and patience through success, failure, and success.

CONTENTS

Chapter 1 Baked into the Batter 1

Chapter 2 Taking Whisks, One Step at a Time 25

Chapter 3 Stepping into Real-World Business 41

Chapter 4 Burnt to a Crisp: Lessons from the School of Hard Knocks 55

Chapter 5 Dough or Die: The Bar, the Battle, and the Breakthrough 75

Chapter 6 The Cookie Crumbles, and Then You Bake Another Batch 97

Chapter 7 The Birth of Boozy Cookies (And the Taco Truck That Started It All) 121

Chapter 8 Hand-Mixed and Heaven-Sent: How Small Beginnings Become Big Miracles 143

Chapter 9 Sweeter Together 159

Chapter 10 The Kind of Magic You Can Taste 181

Acknowledgments 193

Chapter 1

BAKED INTO THE BATTER

There's a rhythm to the way some people move through the world, a kind of cosmic jazz that doesn't follow a chart but still finds its beat.

That rhythm carried me too. I was elbow-deep in flour and Hot Cheeto dust, chasing a flavor I couldn't quite pin down, sealing cookie bags with a borrowed hair straightener that smelled of burnt bangs and ambition.

What came before this moment? A full-blown circus of side hustles and big ideas. Breakfast joints, a pawnshop, an arcade—my childhood came with punch clocks and fryer grease, DJ booths and bingo halls. My parents didn't just raise me; they handed me a front-row seat to the wildest business school Alaska had to offer. So, no, the hustle wasn't new. This time, it just came with sugar on top.

I was born in Lewiston, Idaho, a quiet town with vast skies and working-class grit. Lewiston wasn't the kind of place people moved to chase big dreams. It was steady, humble, and simple in all the ways that made sense . . . until it didn't.

I was still in diapers when things started to slip. My dad was running his own construction company back then, doing everything he could to keep up. But the work slowed, the bills piled up, and, eventually, it all collapsed. They nearly filed for bankruptcy. Instead of walking away, though, my dad picked up the phone. He called every person he owed and promised to make it right. He wasn't going to leave anyone hanging.

No one really knew what the next move would be. Then one of my dad's friends came back from Alaska with a paycheck from the oil field, $700 for just one week of work. Suddenly, a path forward emerged. They could take it, but only if they were willing to leave behind everything they knew. And they were.

They packed what they could: blankets, dishes, tools, whatever would fit. At a Ford dealership, a salesman cut them a deal on a brand-new truck. Then they bolted a camper onto the back, just big enough to sleep in and barely enough to live in. Jay, the second oldest of my four brothers, helped load boxes alongside his wife, Marta, who was pregnant at the time.

I was a year and a half. Sam, my closest sibling in age, was a year older than I was. Andy, the third oldest, was already a teenager. None of us really knew what was happening. We just climbed in and headed north, tracing the Alcan Highway through Canada, pulling away from the only life we knew with nothing but faith and the wild hope of starting over.

After about a week on the road, we pulled into Kenai, a small town tucked between mountains and water. We moved into a two-bedroom apartment, a plain, tight space in a building that, years later, would become Wildwood Prison. It wasn't much, but it was a beginning.

In Alaska, "normal" looks a little different. Summers brought endless daylight, the kind that stretched into midnight and beyond. People taped foil to their windows just to get some sleep, since blackout curtains weren't really a thing back then. And in the winter, the script is flipped. Two or three hours of sunlight was all we got. We didn't complain, though. We just adapted.

And that's exactly what my parents did with everything. They were serial entrepreneurs, though I doubt they'd ever call themselves that. For them, it was simple: See a need, fill it, then move to the next. Over the next 20 years, they opened more than 22 different businesses.

At first, though, it was just about staying afloat. My dad worked "on the slope," as everyone called it, most likely for Tesoro. He'd go up for his shifts, then return home to help my mom pay down what they owed. On one of those trips home, he decided to send her to auction school.

She went, and she came back as the first female auctioneer in the Northwestern states. That accomplishment changed everything. They launched Sally's Auction Company, and soon my mom was running auctions in both Kenai and Soldotna. The towns were twin cities, each with about 2,500 to 3,000 people. They shared geography but carried a rivalry that came alive in schools and sports, and now in bidding wars.

Her first auction brought in $3,000. She came home, spread the cash across the bed, and praised God for blessing her life. A few days later, she passed a narrow storefront tucked beside the movie theater. The awning was faded, the door crooked, but the place carried that specific hum of a space waiting for someone to believe in it. She walked

in, rented it, and named it The Peanut Gallery, a neighborhood variety shop filled with Alaskan gifts, sweets, and a handful of fun odds and ends.

What I didn't know until recently, something my dad shared as if it weren't the hinge of the whole story, was that her parents had passed away around that time and left her a small amount of money. It wasn't much, but it gave her a little wind at her back. That small inheritance, paired with grit and faith in God, made that first storefront possible.

And just like that, the current began to pull us forward.

Five years later, that little shop changed hands again. This time, it went to a woman named Kathryn, who saw the advertisement in the local newspaper and ended up buying it from my mom. At the time, my mom had no idea she was doing business with someone who would eventually become a part of our family. Aaron, Kathryn's grandson, was just a kid then. I wouldn't meet him until years later, and I certainly had no idea I would end up marrying him.

Meanwhile, my mom kept going. That little shop had opened a door, and she was already searching for the next one to walk through.

On a trip to Soldotna, she spotted a small candy store tucked into the front of a local bowling alley. She didn't know if it was available. She didn't ask. She simply did what she had done once before: walked in, claimed the space as if it already belonged to her, and turned the lights on. The place was tiny, with just three tables and a counter lined with 10 barstools, but she had a vision, and that was all she needed to make it real.

She installed a grill and launched her next idea: a two-for-five-dollar breakfast. She named it Sourdough

Another full house at Sourdough Sal's.

Sal's, inspired by her growing obsession with Alaska's gold rush. She read books about history, tested recipes, and baked sourdough bread every morning in old coffee cans. Each loaf rose with that same stubborn hope she carried into every venture.

The grill sat just behind the counter, allowing customers to sip their coffee while watching their breakfasts come to life. On her first day at Sourdough Sal's in 1978, my mom made $45. Hardly enough to retire on, but more than enough to make her eyes twinkle and her wheels spin.

It was fuel, not for the bank account, but for the engine under her hustle, which never idled for long.

Before the grease from her first batch of hash browns had cooled, she was already eyeing the bowling alley it sat inside. To most people, it was just a cavern of creaky lanes, stale beer, and that weird smell that lives in rental shoes. But to her, it was a blank canvas. She didn't know what a bowling league was, couldn't tell a 10-pin from a turkey, and definitely didn't run it by my dad, who was hundreds of miles away, working up on the slope. She just bought the place.

So when he called to check in, expecting a quick hello and an update on the kids, she said, "Things are good. I just bought the bowling alley."

There was a pause long enough to bowl a full frame.

"You've got to be kidding me," he said. "What are we gonna do with a bowling alley?"

"I don't know," she replied. "But there's a league tonight, and I guess we'll figure it out."

And that was that.

There were no vision boards, nor were there any whiteboard strategy sessions. Just guts, gumption, and a bit of Alaska-sized audacity. When my dad came home, he didn't throw a fit. Instead, he signed up for bowling school (yes, an actual school for bowling mechanics) and learned what it took to keep the place running. That was his style. If something needed to be done, he'd figure it out and get to work.

While he was learning the ropes of lanes and leagues, my mom was knocking down walls, literally. She took out the bowling alley's oversized entryway and filled the space with 12 more tables, stretching the restaurant like it had a second wind.

By the time I was about 10 or 11, I was already learning how to teach people to bowl. Not just how to knock down pins, but how to stand right, breathe right, and roll the ball like they meant it. By 13, I was a certified bowling instructor, fully trained in all the little tricks, like nailing the slide on the approach and putting your thumb up to your nose right after you let go of the ball. I didn't know it then, but I was getting my first taste of what it meant to build something alongside my family, one slippery lane at a time.

And then, because owning a bowling alley and a diner still wasn't enough, she bought the entire building. Not just the business but the whole mini mall, the stubborn, lopsided, fluorescent-lit stretch of storefronts.

And just like that, the venture began to snowball.

One of her first new ventures was a pawnshop called

Sam's Pawn Shop, named after my brother. My dad left the slope for good and stepped in to take over running it. While she slung sourdough and scrambled eggs, he was appraising fishing rods, wedding rings, and whatever else wandered through the door. They had officially become a duo of hustle, one flipping pancakes and the other flipping inventory.

But they weren't done. Not even close.

They looked around town and saw one cold, hard truth: Kids had nowhere to go. There were no hangouts, no safe places to let loose, unless you counted the back of a pickup truck or the shadow of a convenience store. So they built one. A roller rink. They called it KC Fun Factory, a name that sounded like it came wrapped in bubblegum and neon lights—exactly right for what they had in mind. And then, because what's a roller rink without an arcade, they opened one of those too. They called it Storman Norman's, named after my dad, who had officially become the patron saint of the side hustle.

Eventually, they added a radio booth above the roller rink, KSLD and KKIS, a little broadcasting loft with a big personality.

Between the rink, the restaurant, the pawnshop, and the arcade, all of us had a role. We DJ'd. We handed out roller skates. We flipped burgers, swept floors, ran the token counter, restocked candy, refilled soda syrups, changed light bulbs, wiped down tables, untangled cords, replaced batteries, tested mics, counted change, cleaned bathrooms, restocked napkin dispensers, hauled garbage, chased loose quarters, calmed crying kids, fetched lost shoes, and made sure the music never stopped. Lucy, my niece, stuck with the DJing. She's now the number one DJ in Alaska. But we all showed up. We all kept it moving. And by the time it was all in full swing, we weren't just part of the operation; we were baked into the batter.

By now, the mini mall didn't feel like a mall. It had morphed into something more like a living organism: part business complex, part community playground, part fever dream fueled by sourdough and sheer willpower. Sourdough Sal's. Storm'n Norman's. KC Fun Factory. Sam's Pawn Shop. Each one had its own personality, yet all were stitched together with the same thread: family sweat, duct tape ingenuity, and my mom's unshakable imagination.

And the sprawl kept growing.

They added a Speedy Lube for the oil-thirsty vehicles of Soldotna; Klondike Chicken for the deep-fried faithful; a flower shop called Cranberry Merchant because, even among all the grease and neon, my mom still made room for something fragrant and fragile.

Eventually, they gave it all a name: Klondike City. And really, what else could they have called it? My mom loved Alaskan history as if it were a childhood friend, and "Klondike" carried the kind of brass-buttoned charm she could never resist.

The storefronts of Klondike City in all its small-town Alaska glory.

And with charm came drama. Not the soap-opera kind, but the theatrical absurdity that only erupts when small-town politics meet the warped geometry of a family-run bowling alley. Picture this: Somewhere between shoe-spray refills and the eternal mystery of the Tuesday league roster, a conspiracy theory took root in our little town. The scandal? Oil patterns on the lanes. The accusation? That one of my brothers was getting "special treatment." Not just whispered behind hands in the snack bar, but circulated like scripture, an actual petition. Paper. Ink. Sign here if you believe the world is ending because lane six hooks to the left.

I remember holding it in my hands, staring at the absurdity like it had fallen off the back of a UFO. This wasn't the Olympic Trials. It was our family bowling alley. It was where the pins had moods, the jukebox played only songs with emotional baggage, and the ice machine had strong opinions about Tuesday.

My mom, who could handle a grease fire with one hand and balance unpaid invoices with the other, was gutted, not in the dramatic, tear-streaked way, but in the quiet, hollow way that happens when the thing you built from nothing gets mocked by people who've never wielded a mop or closed a register at midnight. Her businesses weren't businesses. They were living, breathing extensions of herself. Equal parts grit, glitter, and divine intervention. And when someone dragged them through the parking-lot mud, it bruised something sacred. Looking back, I thank God this didn't happen in the era of Yelp reviews or Twitter threads. She might've burned the whole internet to the ground.

Not that she ever took slander quietly. If someone came in swinging complaints like wet towels in a locker room, she didn't flinch. She just pointed to the door with the authority of a frontier sheriff and said, "Out." That was her style: direct, swift, final. Banned for life. It didn't matter if you were the mailman, the mayor, or even the fire chief.

Which, by the way, she actually did. She banned the fire chief. That's not hyperbole.

It happened during one of her routine metamorphoses, this time transforming half the bowling alley into a bingo hall. Why not diversify your empire with a dab of dabbers and retirees? The fire chief showed up one day, clipboard in hand and a grimace on his face, and declared she needed to build a fireproof wall between the lanes and the bingo. Said it'd run her a cool hundred grand. She stared at him like he'd suggested installing a rocket launcher. Then, calm as a cat in a sunbeam, she said, "Get out. And don't come back." And he didn't. Because when my mom 86'd someone, it wasn't a suggestion. It was the law. Fire codes be damned.

While she was busy exiling civil servants and turning snack bars into mission control, she had another weapon:

branding. Except she never called it that. To her, it was simply a matter of believing something into existence. One day, she looked at her cinnamon rolls—MASSIVE, GOOEY, UNAPOLOGETICALLY SUGAR DRUNK—and declared them world famous. No marketing research. No focus groups. Just a conviction, loud enough to echo across time zones.

"Mom," I asked, genuinely puzzled, "how do you know they're world famous?"

She didn't even blink. "Because I decided they are," she said. "And who's going to tell me they're not?"

She had a banner made the next day: WORLD FAMOUS CINNAMON ROLLS. No fine print. No qualifiers. Just frosting and faith. And wouldn't you know it? People came. Not just from Anchorage or Wasilla, but from Japan, Germany, and the Lower 48. They came because the sign told them it was worth the trip. Because in her own woolly, wild, and weirdly prophetic way, my mom understood something that most business schools forget to teach: If you say it like you mean it—and back it up with something that tastes like heaven—you don't need a certificate of authenticity. You just need a belief loud enough to shine.

It was brilliant. And a little unhinged. But mostly brilliant. Because what she taught me in that moment, without a TED Talk or a whiteboard, was that greatness doesn't come with permission slips. You claim it, live it, bake it at 375 degrees, drizzle it with icing, and put it on a banner. You don't wait for the world to validate your dream. You serve it hot and dare them not to come back for seconds.

RAISED BY HUSTLE, FUELED BY FAITH

There was a day—probably a Thursday, because Thursdays always needed extra ketchup—when I was standing behind the register at Sourdough Sal's, ringing up a guy who looked like he'd just woken up inside a flannel shirt, and he asked how my day was going. I shrugged. "Could be better," I said, a full-blown brat with a cash drawer.

It wasn't even about him. I think I was mad at my mom, or tired, or 13. But that man was about to get a free side of teenage eye-roll with his eggs. My mom caught it before he could blink.

She pulled me aside, eyes blazing like she'd just deep-fried the truth in a cast-iron skillet.

"I don't care what kind of day you're having. You *never* take it out on a customer. You tell them you're doing great. You smile. You make them want to come back."

And that was it. No lecture, no long talk, just that sharp

slice of clarity. I carried that with me, tucked somewhere between the napkin dispenser and the register tape, long before I understood it was about more than customer service. It was about energy. Presence. Not handing your mess to someone else just because they happened to walk through the door.

By then, I'd already braided cheddar and Swiss into checkerboard ribbons. Not just for decoration (well, yes, for decoration), but also because it made lunch feel like a magic trick. If food didn't look like a party, I wasn't interested. I didn't even know that was branding. I just wanted people to smile before they took a bite.

Mom and Dad had more than 20 businesses going at once, depending on the month and whether the fryers were working. A pawnshop, a flower shop, a chicken place, a roller rink, radio stations, and an ice cream counter tucked next to the arcade—we had it all. I didn't think it was weird. It was like growing up inside a pinball machine powered by espresso shots and duct tape. My mom installed the first espresso machine in Alaska, not because the market demanded it, but because she did. She moved through the world like that, half practicality, half prophecy. If something broke, Dad fixed it. If something didn't exist yet, Mom willed it into being.

When they were too busy to parent in the traditional sense, they handed me and Sam a roll of quarters and said, "Go play." So we did. Hours and hours of *Bubble Bobble*, *Ms. Pac-Man*, and whatever else glowed under the neon inside Storman Norman's, the arcade my mom named after my dad because, in her world, everything was personal. I got so good at those games that by high school, when we had to take a hand–eye coordination test, the results came back saying I could be a surgeon. A surgeon. Because of video games.

Sam and I thought we were cashing in every time they handed us a fresh roll of quarters. We didn't realize the games belonged to Mom. She gave us the coins, and we fed them right back into her machines. She was recycling our childhood into arcade revenue, and we *thanked* her for it. That is elite-level parenting.

But things weren't all fun and neon. Cracks began to show. Not all at once, just little fractures at first. Raised voices behind closed doors. Tense dinners where the clink of silverware filled the silence. Money was usually the topic. Or time. Or the sheer exhaustion of trying to hold up a whole mini mall with nothing but grit and a ticking clock.

Dad wanted family dinners. Mom wanted to open another shop.

It all boiled over during my sophomore year. Mom packed a few bags, moved to Anchorage, and got an apartment. Sam and I stayed with Dad. Andy was already married with kids by then, building a life of his own. But I remember the quiet after she left. The kind that settles in deep and hangs around.

And I remember watching my dad just . . . keep going.

He wasn't the visionary. He was the guy with the wrench. If the bowling machine jammed, he fixed it. If Mom had a new idea, he found a way to bring it to life. He was the one who remembered your dog's name and asked about your grandma's surgery while tightening a loose hinge. People loved him for that.

When Mom left, it was as if he suddenly became captain of a ship he never planned to sail. A dozen businesses, none of which he dreamed up but all of which he kept running.

He leaned on people when he could, but the stress showed. There was no big meltdown, no dramatic final scene. Just the slow unraveling of two people pulling in opposite directions: one chasing presence, the other chasing purpose.

That's who they were. Dad craved home. Mom craved momentum. It's not that she didn't love us. She just loved building things. And sometimes, when you're out trying to hold up half the town, the house quietly slips through your fingers.

I see that pull in myself now, clear as day. I carry my mom's spark, the part that loves dreaming, building, and throwing new ideas against the wall just to see what sticks. But I also carry my dad's heart. I want to be present. I want to show up. I want my people to feel valued and important. And trying to hold both at once? It's not tidy. It's a juggling act most days. But growing up in the middle of their two worlds—one chasing growth, the other craving grounding—taught me how to move between both without dropping everything in the process.

Looking back, I was already living that balancing act before I even knew it had a name. It was baked into the rhythm of our days. That was my childhood. It didn't look like the lemonade stands you see in picture books, with kids perched on upside-down milk crates holding handwritten signs. It looked like real customers, real receipts, and a mom yelling for someone to restock the napkins before the breakfast rush hit. While other kids rode bikes around the cul-de-sac, I was working the register, slicing cheese, or pitching new sundae ideas for our ice cream counter, blissfully unaware that we were literally parked next to a Dairy Queen. I didn't think of it as work, not really. I thought of it as fun, as usual, as just how things were supposed to be. But without even knowing it, I was soaking up everything. I was learning how to communicate effectively with people, how to solve problems, and how to turn a "no" into a "maybe" and a "maybe" into a sale. I wasn't playing house. I was already in business. I just didn't know it yet.

Up until then, church was a nonnegotiable part of life. We were Pentecostal, with services on Wednesday nights, Sunday mornings, and Sunday nights, plus Sunday school. If the doors were open, we were there. And if you were a girl, you were in a dress. No questions asked. If Sam and I were watching TV and two people so much as leaned in for a kiss, we were told to leave the room, as if the screen might start smoldering if we stayed too long. It was strict, serious, and, for me, suffocating. The kind of quiet suffocation you don't notice until someone finally cracks open a window.

By the time high school rolled around, I was already easing away from it. Not from God, but from all the noise that came attached. The judgment, the rules, the theater of holiness, which felt more like a performance than a connection. It didn't speak to me, so I built my own rhythm. I didn't rebel in the traditional sense. I wasn't out drinking or sneaking through windows at night. I just stayed busy. Choir, work, repeat. I liked the structure. I liked doing something with purpose. My schedule was packed, and that was how I liked it. No time to feel boxed in, no space for guilt to sneak in the side door. Life made more sense when I was on the move.

When my parents split up during my sophomore year, church attendance quietly slipped off the calendar. No more four-service weeks. No more itchy dresses or whispered lectures about secular music. Everyone just stopped going. For a while, that silence felt like freedom, a relief I didn't know I needed. But faith has a funny way of hanging on. Even when you think you've walked away, it stays tucked in your coat pocket, showing up in the quiet, in the grit, in the moments you swear you're doing it all alone. It waits, it watches, and sometimes, it sneaks back in through the side door just to remind you it was never really gone.

It wasn't until my mom was gone that I realized how much had stuck. I found some of her journals, filled with prayers in her looping handwriting. She'd write things like, "God, I need ten thousand dollars to pay my taxes by tomorrow, please make it happen." And then, right there in the following entry: "God provided eleven thousand dollars at the last minute." No big reaction. Just a fact. Just faith. That was how she moved through the world.

I didn't know it at the time, but I was absorbing

everything. Her faith. Her audacity. My dad's steadiness. The way they both kept building even after things cracked. They didn't hand me a manual. There weren't sit-down lectures about how to hustle, pray, or make something out of nothing. But they lived it, every single day. In every side gig and sold pawn item. In every midnight diner shift and overdrawn account. In every prayer scribbled between bills, and every receipt stuffed into the junk drawer. I was watching, even when I didn't know I was. Soaking it in like flour into dough, the kind of thing that disappears, but leaves everything changed.

And if you asked me now what I truly carried forward, what stuck after all the burnt toast and whispered prayers, the pawn slips, and tension and drive, it was this: You show up, even when it's hard. You figure it out, even when you're scared. You walk toward the unknown, as if it might actually say yes. You don't wait for clarity. You don't wait for certainty. And you definitely don't wait for permission.

And you wear your lipstick.

At her restaurant, it was part of the dress code. Every woman behind the counter wore it, red or dark pink, with no smudges or excuses. Those were her standards, and now they're mine. I still wear it. Not for anyone else, but for me. Because it completes the look, just as punctuation completes a sentence. It says I'm here. I'm ready. I'm not backing down. It sharpens the edge, draws the line, calls the shot before I even open my mouth.

It was never about vanity. It was about intention. Presence. Pride. Whether you like it or not, the way you walk into a room is the way the world remembers you.

And I plan to be remembered, in full color.

Chapter 2

TAKING WHISKS, ONE STEP AT A TIME

Some businesses are born in boardrooms with latte machines and laminated agendas. Mine was born in the fluorescent-lit jungle of junior high, stitched together with denim, rhinestones, and the kind of blind audacity only a 13-year-old with a glue gun and no concept of scalability could summon. It was bingey. It was chaotic. It was unmistakably Molly.

I wasn't looking to start a business. I was trying to outshine algebra.

It started with a jean jacket and a low-level obsession with personal flair. I didn't want to blend in; I wanted to blaze. So I dragged my seafoam-green-and-pink Caboodle to the kitchen table, pushed aside the saltshaker, and got to work. That table doubled as my design studio and dinner zone, which meant every evening I had to clear off the evidence of my brilliance so we could eat meatloaf like a normal family.

The process was violent, honestly. Each stud had to be forced through layers of denim thick enough to deflect small-caliber bullets, and more often than not, they bit back. My fingers turned into pincushions. I bled, and I rationed Band-Aids. Eventually, I wrapped every fingertip in makeshift armor and pressed on, using a flathead screwdriver I'd pilfered from my dad's toolbox to twist the prongs down and lock them in. It was the kind of hands-on, slightly masochistic work that made me feel like both a warrior and a fashion intern in purgatory.

But the result? A jacket so loud it practically had its own sound system. My name exploded across the back in rhinestones. The collar, cuffs, and sleeves were fully armed and operational. I put that thing on and walked into school, as if I were launching a coup against conformity. Heads turned. Whispers trailed behind me like perfume.

And somewhere between the sparkle and the stab wounds, something inside me woke up.

Did I think I looked amazing? Absolutely. Like a walking disco ball with a grudge and a dream.

One girl—Gwen, bless her—stopped me in the hallway and asked where I bought it. When I told her I made it, she didn't even blink. "Will you make me one?"

I didn't blink either. "Sure. Bring me your jacket. It's twenty-five cents a stud."

Why 25 cents? I couldn't tell you. Maybe it was divine inspiration. Maybe it just sounded grown-up and a little bossy. I had no pricing strategy, no clue what profit margins were, and zero awareness of labor costs. I just liked the way it rolled off my tongue: decisive, confident, official.

Gwen's jacket took me three days to make. Her name was short, just four letters, but I went all in. I gave her the full treatment: name across the back, studs lined up like tiny soldiers, rhinestones everywhere I could reasonably justify them. When I handed it over, she lit up like someone had handed her front-row tickets to destiny.

And just like that, the world tilted, just a little, but enough for me to feel it in my studded fingertips. It wasn't about the 12 bucks, though that felt like a small fortune to a girl still hoarding Lip Smackers and vending machine quarters. It was the fact that something I made with glue, burns, and questionable tools lit someone else up like a marquee. I'd turned a denim jacket into a feeling. That was the real currency.

Then came the ripple.

Word spread fast and sparkly. Three more kids showed up with their jackets in hand and hopeful eyes, as if I were some kind of rhinestone oracle. That brought my client list to four (*four!*), which, in my 13-year-old brain, translated directly into empire status. Forget lemonade stands and babysitting gigs. I was running a haute couture sweatshop out of my bedroom. The carpet was crunchy with glue dots, the air smelled faintly of E6000, and my business plan consisted of vibes and bedazzling by moonlight.

Now, here's the thing: I didn't grow up in a house full of gold stars and refrigerator praise. My parents weren't the type to cheer you on. They weren't cruel, they were just busy, distracted, always building something. If I launched a jacket business or a school fundraiser or a plan to colonize Mars, I think the most I'd get would be a blink and a "Huh. That's nice."

And my siblings? Oh, we ran our household like it was an Olympic sport, and the event was "Who Said It First?" I'd have an idea, speak it into the room, and within minutes, one of my brothers would echo it slightly louder, slightly smugger, and suddenly it was theirs. My mom would beam. I'd smolder. This happened so often that I briefly considered charging *them* 25 cents a thought.

So, when someone, anyone, did see value in something that was unmistakably mine? That stuck. That mattered.

By high school, my creativity had leveled up. I became obsessed with fashion. Not the runway kind, the hallway kind. The "let me wear this strange skirt with these cowboy boots and this fringe scarf and make it feel like art" kind.

In my junior year, I made a pact with myself: no outfit repeats. Not even once. If I'd worn that shirt with those jeans before, something had to change: different shoes, an added layer, anything to make it feel fresh. I wasn't doing it for attention. I just loved the process. There was something deeply satisfying about pulling together an outfit that didn't exist the day before and realizing it somehow fit, not just on my body, but on who I was becoming. Some days it came together fast. Other days, it meant digging through the back of my closet like an archaeologist in a polyester jungle. But when it worked, when I found a piece I truly loved, or a combination that surprised me, it gave me a lift I couldn't explain. The outside started to catch up to the inside, and I carried that feeling with me all day.

By senior year, school dances had started to feel like reruns. The same two dress shops, the same sea of satin, the gym transformed into what looked like a rerouted bridal expo, with every girl pretending not to notice that someone else was wearing her dress in a slightly different shade. There wasn't much room to feel original, and everyone knew it.

We didn't have the internet back then, but we had magazines, and I had ideas. I tore through my stack of *Seventeens*, circling names like Jessica McClintock, Gunne Sax, Morgan & Co., any designer whose dresses had structure, a little story, something that felt like more than fabric on a hanger. I sat down and wrote them letters, real ones, not emails or order forms, but handwritten notes folded into envelopes with a couple of stamps and a quiet kind of boldness. I told them about our town, about the gym that turned into a sea of near-matching dresses every dance, and about the girls who wanted to feel like they were wearing something that spoke to them, something uniquely theirs. I asked if they'd be willing to sell me just one of each style, no duplicates, no bulk orders, just enough to give every girl her own moment.

And to my surprise, they said yes.

The catalogs arrived like little books of possibility, thick with pages of silk, tulle, and imagined futures. During lunch, I'd spread them across the cafeteria table like maps, and soon enough, girls would gather around, flipping through the pages and pointing to the one that made them light up, as if their whole body said, "*Yes, this is the one.*" Once someone chose a dress, it was off the table, no repeats, no doubles. That was the promise. And they trusted me to keep it.

I can still see it, the gym glowing under strings of white lights, music humming through the walls, and then Carol stepping in, wearing the deep emerald gown we'd picked out together. It caught the light in a way that made her glow from the inside out, like she knew she'd nailed it before she'd even said a word. She walked in with the kind of ease that made heads turn, not because she was loud, but because she didn't have to be.

And then Diane, across the room in that soft lace dress, almost vintage in feel, the kind of gown that made her look like she'd floated out of another era. Her hair pinned up, her posture graceful, she moved through the room as if she were in on some secret the rest of us hadn't figured out yet. No one else looked like her. No one came close. For a second, I forgot the hustle, the catalogs, the rush, and just watched her shine.

The word spread like gossip at a beauty salon, quick, bright, and impossible to contain. Girls started getting asked where they found their dresses, and when they said my name, Molly Blakeley, more came. Like clockwork, like migration. One turned into three, three turned into ten, and before I knew it, I was taking orders faster than I could explain what I was actually doing. It didn't feel like a business yet. Not officially. But it had a pulse. It was moving.

Then came the first wedding. One of the girls I'd dressed for prom found out she was expecting, and when she and her longtime boyfriend decided to get married, I offered to help. No big pitch, no business plan—just a simple, "Hey, I got you." We flipped back through the catalogs, but this time with a new kind of glow in mind. She found a dress that made her eyes light up. We also selected gowns for the bridesmaids. It was simple. It was sweet. And it stuck; they're still married.

That was the moment I felt the shift, not a bang, not a headline, but a quiet pivot from "I'm helping" to "I'm building." It wasn't just a fluke or a fun little side hustle. It was taking shape, finding legs, and revealing a surprising amount of heart. Not by accident, but by instinct. By consistency. And by the quiet, stubborn belief that when you give something your complete care, real care, not just lipstick-and-clipboard effort, it often grows beyond what you imagined.

And while the dress orders picked up, so did everything else. I stayed busy, like seven jobs at once. I went to school part-time, leaving by 11 AM, and then it was a full sprint until bedtime. Waitressing. Teaching roller skating. Closing the arcade. Inventing sundaes behind the ice cream counter. Cleaning houses. Cooking for a woman with MS who used a wheelchair, volunteering with seniors, and helping local choirs. If there was something that needed to be done, I found a way to fit it in.

People always asked how I kept it up, but the truth was that I needed it. My mom had left, and I didn't want to sit at home staring at the empty spaces she'd left behind. My dad was grieving, and I didn't know how to help. So I filled every hour I could. Movement became my medicine. Busyness kept the ache at bay. And somehow, I still made the honor roll.

Choir was my one still point in the midst of it all. I didn't think much about it at the time; I just knew I loved it. Singing gave me a place to exhale.

People had things to say. Some called me a go-getter. A few probably thought I was too much. But I wasn't spoiled; I was shaped. I'd grown up watching the waitresses at

Sourdough Sal's run the place like it was mission control. They moved quickly, spoke candidly, and never let a ketchup bottle go to waste. They didn't complain. They didn't quit. They just worked.

And I loved them for it. I loved the rhythm of it all: the clatter of dishes, the buzz of voices, the feeling that I mattered because I was part of the hum. That's where I learned how to move with purpose, how to build from the ground up, and maybe, most of all, how to dream while wiping down tables.

JUNIOR MISS AND THE ACCIDENTAL CROWN

I was a senior in high school, and Soldotna's Junior Miss competition was *the* event. Every girl wanted in. Big audience, big stage, and the kind of spotlight that made your eyeliner nervous.

Technically, it was a scholarship program, which sounded good to adults. But I wasn't in it for college money; I didn't even want to go to college. I signed up to win the talent portion of the competition. That was the goal. That was the mission. I wanted someone to look at me and say, "*You're the best talent around.*"

I'd already been in All-State and All-Northwest Choir, but those came with polite applause and certificates that ended up in the back of a drawer. I wanted a real win. One with a microphone and a standing ovation that rattled your ribs.

The rehearsals were intense. Three months of synchronized spins, choreographed smiles, and interviews that felt like verbal gymnastics in a prom dress. There were 32 of us in total, 16 girls from Soldotna and 16 from Kenai, and the stakes felt sky-high in our little town. Most of the girls took it seriously. *Very* seriously. Straight-A students with color-coded planners, practiced answers, and posture that said, "*I'm here to win.*" They probably fell asleep to the sound of their own interview questions echoing in their heads.

But my best friend Martina and I? We were just along for the ride. Neither of us had the grades to win, which made it all the more enjoyable. No pressure, no pretending, we actually got to enjoy it. People kept asking if I thought I had a shot, and I'd just laugh. *Not even close*. I was there to sing my heart out, soak in the chaos, and—if I was lucky—leave someone thinking, *That girl's got something.*

And because I wasn't chasing the crown, I had room for everything else. I made little handmade gifts for the girls, the volunteers, and probably even the guy who set up the folding chairs. Somewhere between the rehearsed smiles and the jazz hands, it stopped feeling like a competition and started to feel like a community, stitched together with glitter, bobby pins, and shared snacks from someone's mom's minivan. I didn't want it to end.

For my big moment onstage, I sang a medley of *God Bless the USA* into *America the Beautiful*. And because this was Soldotna, Alaska, we borrowed the biggest American flag we could get our hands on from the local car lot, obviously. When that flag dropped behind me, it didn't feel like a high school talent competition anymore. It felt like an *event*. Loud, proud, unapologetic. Just the way I liked it.

And just like that, it was over.

I walked offstage feeling like I'd already gotten everything I came for. I'd sung. I'd had a blast. I finished my moment. Now it was time to settle in, clap for the real winners, and maybe hit Sourdough Sal's after just to celebrate surviving the night.

And then they dimmed the lights. They brought us all back out, the full lineup of smiling girls, standing shoulder to shoulder across the stage, waiting. The air felt heavier somehow. The hush of the crowd, the bright lights, that weird mix of nerves and glitter hanging in the air like hairspray. It was the part where they started handing out awards.

I grinned, fully relaxed, certain my job for the night was done, until they called my name.

Poise and Appearance.

"Candidate #1, Molly Blakeley."

Wait, what?

Then the Interview.

"Candidate #1, Molly Blakeley."

Okay. Now this was getting weird.

Then, the Onstage Question.

"Candidate #1, Molly Blakeley."

By then, you can see it all over my face in the VHS tape, that slow, stunned expression, like surely someone had mixed up the scorecards.

And then, for Talent. The one I actually came for, the one I wanted.

"Candidate #1, Molly Blakeley."

Never, not for a second, did it cross my mind that winning all those categories might mean I'd win the whole thing. That wasn't the plan. That wasn't even possible in my brain. I was just thrilled to be standing there, holding more than I ever expected, already floating on cloud nine.

But then the big one. The overall winner.

Molly Blakeley!! Then silence.

Not the electric, cheer-ready silence. The kind that stretches long enough to wonder if the emcee had forgotten how to read or time itself had just stalled.

And then it hit me.

My name. My *actual* name.

I didn't move. I didn't blink. Somewhere there's a VHS tape of me standing there, arms limp, mouth open, looking like I'd just been named Homecoming Queen in a town I didn't even live in. I walked across that stage like I was in someone else's dream. No sparkly crown, just a massive medallion like I'd won Olympic gold in Unexpected Victories.

And a scholarship. A full ride to any college in Alaska, Idaho, Oregon, or Washington. Which was hilarious, because I still had zero plans to go.

Looking back, I think that's when the room got a little quieter around me. Not in a mean way. Not even in a noticeable way at first. Just different. Like everyone was trying to catch up to what had just happened. I'd spent three months with these girls. Cheering them on, making little handmade gifts, saying (loudly, often) that I wasn't there to win anything but the talent portion. I think they believed me. I believed in myself. But there I was, standing with it all.

Official portrait from Molly Blakeley's Junior Miss victory.

Most of them had wanted the scholarship. I hadn't. And I guess that made the whole thing land differently for some people. Funny how fast things can shift. But I was still standing there, holding the medallion, holding the moment, feeling like maybe life was a little wilder, and a little less predictable, than I'd ever given it credit for.

After all the photos, flowers, and chaos, one of the

organizers pulled me aside. She still had that post-show glow about her, but there was something in her face, that look adults get when they know something about you that you haven't quite figured out yet. She smiled and said, "You didn't think you could win. You didn't have the grades. But we just knew you would."

That line settled somewhere deep in my rib cage, like a truth I'd always hoped was real but never quite had permission to believe. Because here's the thing nobody really tells you growing up: You don't have to tick every box to land somewhere big. You don't have to be the most polished, the most perfect, or the most expected person in the room. Sometimes you just have to show up exactly as you are, loud, vibrant, imperfect, and let the rest work itself out, even if you're in a borrowed dress, even if no one sees it coming. Especially then.

Afterward, we went to Sourdough Sal's, of course. Where else would we go? That was the place—the place where everything good got celebrated in Soldotna. Mom and Dad were beaming. People came over to hug me, high-five me, tell me they knew it all along, which was funny, because *I* sure hadn't.

Chapter 3

STEPPING INTO REAL-WORLD BUSINESS

After high school, I followed love all the way to San Diego. His name was Chad, and he was the kind of small-town Alaska boy that girls like me didn't just crush on; they wrote their future last names in the margins of their notebooks over and over. We met at a school dance—a lock-in, no less—where the adults literally locked us inside from 7 PM to 7 AM, like hopeful inmates of hormonal possibility. He was a hockey star, a football player, and just about the cutest boy this Soldotna girl had ever seen. And I fell. Hard.

We were inseparable after that. Chad bowled where I worked. He waited for me after shifts. He was the first boy who ever looked at me like I might very well be the main event in his life. He was my biggest cheerleader, forever pretending to faint when I got dressed up. And when he proposed to me right there at my favorite Chinese restaurant, with a boom box blaring Bryan Adams, I said yes, as if it were the only word I'd ever learned.

Before long, we were packing up our little Alaska love story and trading snow boots for flip-flops. Chad settled into life as a Marine at Camp Pendleton, and I landed a job managing a party supply store in San Diego called Party Land. It was the kind of place that sold everything from helium balloons to disco ball centerpieces, and I thrived there. The owner, Shelly, hired me on the spot after I told her, straight-faced, "You'd be dumb not to hire me. I'm going to make you a lot of money." And I did.

California was a world away from the frosty stillness of Alaska. For a season, it felt like magic, the dizzy, giddy, butterflies-in-your-gut kind of magic. But real life has a knack for showing up uninvited, unimpressed by butterflies and boom boxes, and bringing along its less glamorous companions: routine and reality. We were young. And sometimes young love, for all its sparkle, just isn't built for the long haul. I had gained weight, and I could feel the distance growing between us, not just in inches or looks, but in the way he stopped seeing me the way he used to. And then, like dropping a glass on tile, everything shattered. I found out Chad had strayed. Complete devastation hardly begins to describe it. We tried counseling, but he'd already made up his mind. He had already moved on.

So I gave my boss, Shelly, six weeks' notice at Party Land and started clocking serious overtime, helping her transition and training the new manager. When I wasn't at work, I holed up in the spare room of our apartment near Camp Pendleton, a room that slowly turned into my own personal heartbreak observatory. Most nights, Chad would call her. Laugh with her. Talk to her as if there weren't a marriage dissolving just 10 feet away. And I'd lie there, listening, inhaling every syllable like secondhand smoke.

It wasn't the kind of heartbreak they write ballads about. It was slower. Quieter. Like a weight pressing on my chest, turning breath into effort. But I kept showing up, for work, for myself, because I didn't know what else to do.

Still, even in the fog of all that loss, there was this stubborn little echo of the girl I used to be. The one who didn't just sing while doing dishes; she sang like the dishes were lucky to have her. I used to dream of Broadway auditions, the kind with sweaty palms, real casting directors, and maybe even my name on some cheap marquee blinking like it meant something. But love is weird. Love can be sticky. When Chad and I got married, I folded that dream up like a letter I'd never send and tucked it into the back of my mind. At the time, it felt like loyalty, like loving someone enough to gently tuck your wildest parts into a drawer marked "later."

And for a while, that was okay. I loved being his wife. I loved our life. It was steady in its own way, simple and sure. And I poured myself into it with everything I had. But when it all came apart, I packed up what little I had left—a few suitcases and a gut full of grief—and flew back to Alaska. My mom had an apartment with a roommate waiting.

PUTTING THE PETAL TO THE METAL

With my heart a little battered but my ego somehow still kicking, I took a job managing the floral department at Safeway. And that, dear reader, is where I went full peacock. I color-coordinated the risers with plants, flowers, and balloons. I built balloon arches like a one-woman

Macy's parade float committee. And then I discovered the loudspeaker.

"Good afternoon, Safeway shoppers! Make your way to the flower department where you can bring your wife home beautiful roses for just $9.99. Go from a zero to a hero! I'm Molly, the floral manager, and I'm here to help!"

It sparked like wildfire. Soon enough, Dianne in the bakery caught on. Just like that, Safeway turned into my own small-town version of *Saturday Night Live*, complete with unscripted banter and a captive grocery store audience. Customers ate it up. Management? Well, not all of them were fans.

Which brings me to Dave. The assistant manager-in-training with slicked-back brown hair, glasses that caught the fluorescent light just so, and a walk like he was late to every emergency happening in aisle five. He wore his white button-down shirt and black pants like armor and moved through Safeway as if order itself depended on him, like every step counted toward some invisible promotion. Fast. Focused. Determined to keep order in a world of wayward grocery carts and rogue floral arches. Most days, he'd stay upstairs, perched in the glass-walled office that overlooked the whole store, like a grocery store lighthouse keeper. But when he descended, it was with purpose. And every single time he passed my floral display, he'd bump something—a vase, a balloon, a little piece of my patience—then bark, "Molly, grab a broom," like that was the whole job description written in Sharpie.

When I finally worked up the nerve to ask for a raise, a whopping $11.20 an hour in 1995, I might as well have asked Dave if I could moonlight as Safeway's CEO. I wasn't just some floral clerk hoping for a handout—I had increased sales by over 110% compared to previous years. And I knew enough to know that even a 2% bump was a big deal in retail. I'd made that department bloom—in every way that counted.

But Dave? He didn't blink. Didn't hesitate. Just hit me with that line like it was policy etched on the side of the building.

"You're at the top of your pay scale," he said. "You'll never make more than you're making right now."

Cue the internal mic drop. If that was the ceiling, then clearly I needed new architecture, something with skylights and potential. I left work that day not just frustrated, but lit up with something that felt suspiciously like direction.

I asked Dad if I could borrow $10,000 on his credit card. He said yes in the way only a dad does when he knows his daughter is either about to build an empire or learn a very expensive lesson. We shook on it like we were closing a deal at the kitchen table, no contracts, no fine print, just faith. And just like that, Molly's Flower Factory was in bloom.

Mom, who had taken back Klondike City after my parents' divorce, had a little space in her building opening up, a sliver of real estate that had once been a flower shop, then briefly a newspaper office, and for a while, nothing but square footage gathering dust. I asked if I could rent it, and Mom, who loved a good business deal the way some people love grandbabies, raised an eyebrow. Sentiment wasn't exactly her currency. But she knew Dad was backing me with his credit card, and money talks, especially to my mother. There were no discounts, no family perks, just straight-up $1,500 a month, like any other hopeful fool trying to turn dreams into rent.

But while that shop was coming to life, so was a whole new chapter I hadn't planned for.

When I moved back to Alaska I rebounded pretty hard and fell for a man who promised me the world. I needed to hear every love bomb song he had to sing. That's where my two girls came along, Emerald first, then Anni. They were my reason and my rhythm in those early years, pure joy even when life around us was complicated.

It was not the best marriage, and took a toll on my daily life, but I was determined to create a life that wasn't defined by what I'd lost but by what I could grow. Somewhere between bottle feedings and nap schedules, that determination took shape as Molly's Flower Factory.

I was juggling more than roses and ribbon. I was building a business while learning how to stand on my own again. Even when it was hard, I never stopped believing that both could bloom.

The sign was up, the rent was due, and there I was, standing in a nearly empty shop with nothing but some bold ideas and a $10,000 gamble riding on my ability to get creative. I didn't have much inventory, so I had to think fast. That's when I came up with the idea for a craft co-op. Local artisans could rent small booths in the shop, pay me rent, and I'd also take a percentage of whatever they sold. It brought energy and people into the space, covered my rent, and, without meaning to, I'd built a pretty savvy little business model. So savvy, in fact, that, eight months in, my mom raised my rent. Note to self: Never let Mom see your profit margins.

The problem wasn't *if* it would work. It was the velocity. Molly's Flower Factory didn't just bloom—it burst into existence like it had something to prove. One month, I was wiring ribbons around tulips and trying to cover rent with booth rentals, and the next, I needed more of everything. More flowers, more hands, more vans, more vases, more hours in the day. Business was booming, but booming comes with its share of bills. And growth, it turns out, isn't free.

Bootstrapping only gets you so far before the boots wear out. I needed capital. Real, grown-up, call-the-bank-and-wear-nice-shoes capital. So I applied for an SBA loan.

Now, I should've been intimidated, a small-town girl walking into a bank asking for a big-girl loan, but instead, I got lucky. Or at least, I got charming. The banker assigned to my file was devastatingly handsome and, I suspect, a little sweet on me. He had this habit of "checking in" more often than necessary, popping by the shop with questions that might've been about the loan, or might've just been about finding an excuse to talk to the girl with the big bouquets and bigger dreams. Whatever his motivation, it worked. The paperwork took time, but when the loan finally came through, I received more than I'd requested. I paid off my dad, stocked up on inventory, and stepped confidently into the next chapter of growth.

And that—unintentionally—became my pattern. I'd build something, breathe life into it, and then either scale it or sell it. Fast starts were my specialty. Not every business lasted forever, but I could get them off the ground like a plane that didn't bother with a runway. Somewhere along the way, I stopped thinking of myself as a shop owner and realized I was a builder. A business developer. A starter of things.

Of course, not everything I touched turned to gold. Some things barely turned at all. And if there's one thing I believe about entrepreneurship, it's this: Never take business advice from someone who hasn't failed. My lessons didn't come wrapped in ribbons—they came wrapped in arguments, rent hikes, poor lighting, and migraine-inducing wall paint.

All the other flower shops were doing what they'd

always done—ordering from the same flower broker in Anchorage, stocking coolers with flowers that had already spent weeks in warehouse purgatory. By the time those blooms landed in a vase, they were halfway to compost. Three days, maybe, before they'd start drooping.

I wasn't about to build my business on leftovers. I skipped the middleman entirely and went directly to the growers, bringing in roses from Ecuador, tulips from Holland, and everything else fresh off the farm and full of life. These weren't flowers that needed to be babied into lasting a few days. They came in bold, breathed deeply, and stuck around for weeks, holding their color and shape as if they had something to prove.

Still, having the best flowers wasn't enough if no one knew about them. I needed people to experience the difference firsthand. So I designed arrangements that were impossible to ignore, big, theatrical, and full of personality. Each one was wrapped in ribbons, exploding with color, and intentionally placed in the most visible spots I could find. I donated them to banks, car dealerships, and other places where the lighting was harsh, the furniture neutral, and the impact immediate. Next to each bouquet, I'd leave a stack of business cards, no pitch, no pressure, just a quiet suggestion with a loud visual.

It didn't take long for the results to speak for themselves. Within a few months, one of the two well-established flower shops in town, 15 years of business behind it, closed its doors. The other came sniffing around, asking where I was sourcing my flowers. I smiled, said nothing, and let them wonder. Trade secret. The truth was, no one else had thought to break the chain. They were too used to doing it the old way to imagine that something better might actually work.

And then there was my van. This was way before people started wrapping their cars in flashy graphics—back when the boldest move a business might make was slapping a square magnet on the doors. But I wasn't interested in subtle. I took my perfectly ordinary minivan and turned it into a floral parade float on wheels—something between the Scooby-Doo Mystery Machine and a mobile revolution. "Flower Power" stretched across the hood like a declaration of joy, while "We Put the Petal to the Metal" shouted from the back in unapologetic lettering. I told the decal guy I wanted people to drive by, squint hard, and ask, "What the hell was that?!" And they did. Heads turned. Conversations started. That van wasn't just transportation. It was my billboard, my brand, and my very loud calling card.

Eighteen months after opening, I sold Molly's Flower Factory for $100,000, ten times what I'd borrowed to launch it. I didn't even have to list it. Two offers came in the same day, and I accepted the one from Tammy, my designer and right hand from the beginning. She knew the shop inside and out and understood its worth, not just on paper, but in spirit. Selling to her wasn't just a business decision. It was a passing of the torch to someone who had helped shape the fire.

That sale was more than a payday. It was my first exit, my first real win, and the moment I saw what could happen when you lead with vision, trust your instincts, and refuse to do things the way they've always been done. I had built something from scratch, made it thrive, and let it go while it was still in full bloom. That kind of win doesn't just shift your bank account; it shifts your sense of what's possible.

And to think, it all started because Dave told me I'd never make more than $11.20 an hour.

Thanks, Dave. Truly.

Chapter 4

BURNT TO A CRISP

Lessons from the School of Hard Knocks

Hope is a tricky landlord. It hands you the keys with a wink, charges full rent by the second month, and won't fix the leak dripping self-doubt onto your carefully arranged display of optimism. Still, you move in. Rearrange the furniture of your ambition. Light a candle that smells like second chances and pretend not to hear the floorboards creak under the weight of déjà vu.

That's about where I was, fresh off selling Molly's Flower Factory, feeling the faint buzz of momentum, and trying to find a rhythm in a life that was suddenly very full. I was still catching my breath from everything that had just unraveled: the cross-country move, the end of a marriage, the fast-forward into motherhood, and somehow, already stumbling headfirst into business ventures like the universe had me on a subscription plan for unexpected opportunities.

Let's just admit up front: This chapter doesn't follow a clean storyline. It veers. It stumbles. It lurches forward in heels too high for the terrain. If you're looking for a neat arc or a heroine who rises from the ashes with perfect timing and a personal brand, you might want to skip ahead. What you're about to get is a woman dragging her smudged résumé through a chicken-scented gift shop, turning a pawnshop into a cabaret, and launching a roller rink while holding a baby and watching the floor fall out, literally and emotionally.

Some stories don't arc so much as taper, closing not with applause, but with a set of keys handed over, a door locked for the last time, a name scraped off a window. This chapter is full of those endings. Some clean, some sticky. Some were made in strength, while others came from sheer exhaustion. But each one, in its own sideways way, is a kind of resolution. Not the sort that earns headlines or hashtags, but the quiet kind, a decision to leave, to sell, to start again with whatever scraps you've got left. It's less about the drama and more about the after: what you learn to carry, what you finally lay down, and how you come to trust yourself to build again even when your hands are still shaking.

SASSAFRAS & THE GIFT SHOP GUILLOTINE

After I sold Molly's Flower Factory, I jumped into a new venture with three women who, on paper, looked like the dream team: veteran business owners from Soldotna, successful in their own right, and equally ambitious. We called it Sassafras, a gift shop filled with beautiful decor and high hopes. The idea was simple: Each of us would work two days a week, and we'd close on Sundays. In theory, it was breezy. In practice, it was a room full of alpha women arguing over which shade of cream was "warmer" and whether Norah Jones or Stevie Nicks belonged on the speakers. The bickering started before we even opened the doors. Dread crept in before we ever cut the ribbon.

Still, the store opened and in its first month, it pulled in around $45,000. But here's the kicker: 70% of the sales were mine. That didn't go over well. Jealousy has a scent, and it was starting to stink up the shop.

If you're bringing in most of the sales and still getting

treated like the problem, it's not you; it's the room. Don't stick around just because you helped paint the walls.

Later, I heard they kicked out another partner. Eventually, only one of the original four was left standing. Naturally, the first thing she did was paint all the walls white, because nothing says "vision" like scrubbing away every trace of personality. Soon enough, the whole shop went under.

THE PERFECT PRESENT: HANDLE WITH CARE

After Sassafras, I was burnt toast: emotionally charred, spiritually undercooked, and trying to make something, anything, out of what was left. I had survived the four-headed co-owner disaster, walked away from a business I helped start, and tried to smile while the people I trusted cashed in on the work I had poured myself into. And because, apparently, I had not learned my lesson yet, I poured what little I had left into a fading roller rink, baby on my hip, determination in my eyes, only to be handed a goodbye wrapped in a property sale. I was exhausted, humiliated, and angry. Beneath all that mess, something in me flared up and hissed, *Oh yeah? Watch this.*

Still bruised but not broken, I opened a tiny shop, a quirky little gift basket store where baskets hung from the ceiling and customers could fill their own creations. I named it The Perfect Present, which felt like a joke. It was far from perfect and definitely not a present. The place used to be a fried chicken joint, and if you have ever tried to open a boutique inside a poultry crime scene, you know that no amount of Febreze can erase the scent of deep-fried history baked into the walls.

But I was determined. I had baskets hanging from the ceiling, cute little tags with sassy notes, and shelves full of gifts that said, "Look, I care, but I also had ten bucks and five minutes." It was cozy, colorful, and creative. It was me, if "me" had recently been flattened by betrayal and was trying to tape herself back together with decorative ribbon and seasonal merchandise. I think I was trying to give myself the gift I wished someone else would hand me. Unlike Sassafras, no one was plotting against me. No whispering. No power plays. The only person who could ruin this one was me, and strangely enough, that felt like freedom.

Truth was, I did not open that shop because I had a genius plan. I opened it because I needed to prove I could still build something on my own. No partners. No politics. No one rearranging my vision behind my back. Just me, my pride, and a lingering cloud of emotional jet fuel. I told myself I was rebuilding, but I was really running: from disappointment, from failure, from the parts of me that did not know how to rest.

My body had other plans. It began to rebel in steady, insistent ways: fatigue that would not lift, aches that did not make sense, a heaviness I could not shake, and then my vision began to blur. I had to get glasses.

Part of that weight came from home.

I will not lay it all out here, but I will say this. Home was not a place of rest. My marriage was fraying in ways that shook me to my core. There were cracks in the communication, gaps where trust used to live. And still, I stayed. Eight years of trying to hold a family together with sheer will and a stomach full of knots. I stayed for my daughters. I stayed because I thought that was the right thing to do.

I stayed even as it made me sick.

Not all at once, at first. Just a flicker here and there: a pressure behind my eyes, a buzzing beneath my skin, headaches that drilled behind my temples and left me blinking through fog. My body was blinking red, filing complaints no one else could see.

The migraines, which I had battled for more than a decade, began to come harder and faster until I found myself in the hospital month after month, receiving injections just to make the pain manageable. The darkness behind my eyes deepened, and my vision blurred more often.

And here is the truth I did not understand then. I thought I was just tired. I thought I was built to handle it. I wince now every time I look back, because I did not see what was happening. I was too busy being unstoppable. Too sturdy. Too spark-lit. Too good at adapting to notice my body had filed a complaint and was now staging a full protest. I was addicted to being needed, and I did not know how to stop performing strength, even when it was costing me mine.

What I did not see, what few of us do while we are still mid-sprint, is that even forward motion has a price. I believed I could outwork exhaustion, out-dream it. If I just kept building new things, bold things, things that lit my creative spark, maybe I could outrun whatever was hollowing me out. For a while, it worked. The spark stayed lit, and the ideas kept coming, but creativity lives inside a body, and bodies have limits. Burnout does not always arrive with sirens. Sometimes it moves in disguised as stamina. The truth is, I did not know who I was without the next project to prove it. Slowing down felt like failure. I did not have words for it yet, only a rising sense that the pace was not sustainable, that something essential was leaking out faster than I could refill it. Still, I carried on.

This is usually where the memoir swerves, where the story glosses over what came next. Cue the swelling strings, the mysterious diagnosis, the righteous pivot into reinvention. But that is not this story. Not yet. The drama was not cinematic; it was cellular. No villain was twirling a mustache in the corner. The betrayal was hormonal. The heartbreak was cortisol. I was not fighting a dragon. I was trying to track inventory while dealing with a migraine. You want a climax? Try pretending you are not unraveling while gift-wrapping bath bombs. There are no trophies for this kind of resilience. No hashtags.

Eventually, the symptoms grew louder than my willpower. A string of doctors. A swirl of tests. And finally, a name for the thing that had been hollowing me out: pseudotumor cerebri. A condition that mimics a brain tumor and threatens your vision, just in case the rest of your life had not already blurred at the edges.

My body was producing excess spinal fluid, and with nowhere else to go, it tried to force its way out through my eyes. A normal spinal fluid pressure is around 150. Mine was over 500.

And somewhere in all of this, amid gift baskets and misfiring neurons, a family member who knew both me and my husband asked a question I could not un-hear:

"He's never going to change. Ten years from now, do you still want this life?"

That was it. That was the moment the scaffolding gave way. I had given everything—my health, my sleep, my sense of self—trying to hold the pieces in place. The truth of that question cut through all of it.

So I left.

I kept showing up at the shop. I arranged the baskets. I taped smiles to my face. I held the whole fragile thing together with twine and denial. I told myself it was strength, but really it was fear—the kind that whispers, "Do not stop, or it will all fall apart." Underneath it all, I was learning, slowly and painfully, what kind of strength it takes to walk away even when staying feels noble, and what it means to finally choose yourself.

Eventually, even the hustle lost its shine. I was tired. My body hurt. The shop was cute and clever, but it was barely breaking even, and only because I kept pouring in everything I had. I was not paying myself. I was running on caffeine and adrenaline, masking burnout with bows and merchandise displays.

The truth was, The Perfect Present was not the kind of business I wanted to scale. It was creative, yes, but it was seasonal, labor-intensive, and inventory-heavy. A ton of work for minimal payoff. Once I admitted that to myself, I started looking at the place differently. When someone walked in and offered me $5,000 for the shop, I said yes.

Sometimes the thing you build just to prove you can is the same thing you have to walk away from to prove you should.

THE ALASKA SHOW: WHERE VAUDEVILLE MET THE PAWNSHOP

There's a particular silence that follows upheaval, not peaceful but ringing. After everything fell apart, I went back to Sal's. Not to reclaim anything, just to survive the echo. I managed and waited tables, carried plates and cleared them, moving through the motions and listening for the next right thing to speak up.

It came quietly, like a shift in the air. In the old bowling alley behind Sourdough Sal's, where the lanes had been ripped out and the concrete lay bare, I saw it: a stage that didn't exist yet. Between a tangle of folding chairs and a rack of my parents' pawnshop furs, I could feel the room pulling toward something loud, sparkly, and alive. There was no plan, no pro forma, no guarantee. Just a nudge on the shoulder that dared me to say yes, and I did.

Life never sends one omen when it can send two. Around the same time, my mom hit $50,000 gambling online. I walked into Hooligan's, her rough-edged bar, to say congratulations and gather myself, and there was Aaron, sitting like he had stepped into a story I hadn't written yet. I turned to my friend and said, "I just met my next ex-husband." I was only half joking. Beginnings have a way of looking like interruptions.

Back in the alley, I started building. I called my high school drama teacher, Terri Zopf, the same one who cast me as Frenchie in *Grease* and failed me in tenth-grade English for skipping class. When I reminded her, she didn't hesitate. "No, dear, you failed yourself." Classic Terri. Then I called Yvette, a creative powerhouse who said yes before I finished the sentence, and she brought along one more woman from the local scene. Three of us could sing. One could not, but she sang anyway at full volume and with zero hesitation. The audience thought it was a bit. She thought she was nailing it. We corrected no one. Her joy became one of the best parts of the whole production.

I painted the floor a deep theatrical black that demanded attention, hung curtains, unfolded tables, and raided the pawnshop like it was a fever-dream prop house filled with fur pelts, a dog-eared Iditarod sled, odd signage, and trinkets no one had touched in years. Somehow it worked. The room remembered itself, or maybe it became itself for the first time.

We called it *The Alaska Show*, part cabaret, part comedy, and part dinner theater with a side of unpredictable. I played a flirtatious gold digger who charmed the husbands and lifted the wives' purses for laughs. We sang about heartbreak and no-good exes, leaning into the drama and

winking through the punch lines. The audience howled, and honestly, so did we.

Then came the thunderclap: Hobo Jim, Alaska's balladeer. I asked him to join before I even knew what the show would become. I only knew I wanted his voice in the room. He said yes, and suddenly we had a headliner. Every night we would tip the joke his way, shouting, "That's the guy!" and the place would erupt. He grinned like he had been in on it all along and stepped straight into the legend everyone already believed.

Behind the curtain, it was joyful chaos. We served a four-course dinner between costume changes and lipstick touch-ups: a salad with whatever Alaskan berries we could find, chowder thick enough to hold a spoon upright, and

my mom's halibut Olympia, with the fish dried on paper towels, covered in mayonnaise and cheddar, and baked until it bubbled. Add warm bread and something sweet, then back under the lights. Some nights the food held the show together better than we did, and I wasn't mad about it.

Offstage, life kept moving. Aaron and I got married the way people leap from cliffs, with adrenaline, longing, and faith that the wind will catch you. By spring, I was pregnant again, one more heartbeat in the mix and one more reason to keep building a life that worked. Rest wasn't my language then. Keeping the lights on was.

Me and Aaron on our wedding day.

Every crowd had its own weather. Some nights we leaned into local jokes. Others ended in a spontaneous line dance. We adjusted on the fly, depending on the mood and whether the chowder boiled over. It wasn't flawless, and that was the charm. A kind of flashlight theater alchemy turned a hollow room behind Sourdough Sal's into a beating heart.

Each week I handed Terri her check, the same woman who once red-penned my grammar now belting a ballad in a feather boa from a box labeled "misc." The seats filled, the lights held, and somehow it worked. When summer ended, the season paused and I moved on to the roller rink. Sequins traded for skates, a new rhythm to learn. But *The Alaska Show* stayed tucked behind my ribs like a secret. I was lucky to live, and Hobo Jim never left my orbit. He grounded the whirlwind.

Here's what I learned in that back-alley theater: Sometimes the best returns don't show up on a balance sheet. Saying yes to what doesn't make sense on paper gave me joy, connection, and momentum I could feel in my bones, the kind that lingers after the laughter fades and follows you into the next venture. Numbers matter, but they are not the only measure. The room tells you when you have built something that matters.

We were scrappy, loud, half-organized, and fully in it. With mismatched props, homemade chowder, and a room that used to be a bowling alley, we made a night people still talk about. That was the magic. We caught it, just for a while, and I am glad I said yes.

So, what happened next? Life kept moving after *The Alaska Show*, reshaping itself in a way that felt steady and full of possibility. I gave birth to Luke, a brand-new heartbeat right in the center of everything I was rebuilding, and his arrival shifted the whole rhythm of my days. He brought a clear sense of purpose, the kind that strengthens your steps and sharpens your focus. Holding him, I felt more rooted and more ready to shape a life with real footing beneath it.

And once that feeling took hold, I put it to work. Stability, in my world, has never been about slowing down. It has always come from creating something with my own hands and turning motion into momentum. So I took over the roller rink and poured myself into it. I painted the walls with color and numbers so schools could use it for educational field trips, and the place started filling with kids, parents, and a kind of energy that felt both wild and productive.

Somewhere in the middle of that hustle, the roller derby team was born. Alaska's very first. Not the modern, rulebook version, but pure 1970s mayhem with derby names, fishnets, and a live band playing inside a chain-link cage while the crowd threw beer at us from the sidelines. Foul a player, spin a wheel, and suddenly you were boxing, pillow fighting, or wrestling. It sounds outrageous, and it was, but it also brought the rink to life. We called ourselves the AK Rally Katz, and I skated as Molly Dagger, which felt like its own kind of therapy. It was noisy and rowdy and completely alive, and it kept the whole place rolling.

Life at the rink had me cruising. Peace settled in slowly. The marriage held. The business had legs. The rink was running smoothly, and I didn't expect that to change anytime soon. How it eventually did is a story for later. The kids were growing in ways that made the house feel full again. We had dinners around a table instead of take-out boxes on countertops. There was laughter, the kind that lingers and softens the edges of a long day. I let myself lean into that warmth, grateful for the balance that found its way into our home.

You could call that a happy ending, although it felt more like a long, easy inhale. A pause with room in it. A place to catch my breath before life shifted again. And as I

"Molly Dagger" and the AK Rally Katz, Alaska's first roller derby team, during the early days of their 1970s-style derby revival at the Soldotna roller rink.

moved through it, I felt ready for whatever would show up next. I adapt. I pivot. I roll up my sleeves and keep moving. The next part of life always arrives, sometimes gently and sometimes with force, and I've learned to meet it with steady hands and an open heart.

Chapter 5

DOUGH OR DIE

The Bar, the Battle, and the Breakthrough

She didn't drop it on me like a bomb. It came as an offer. The bar, the restaurant, the 33-room lodge—"You could run it," my mom said, like she was handing me a familiar set of keys.

I hadn't come to Hooligan's out of nowhere. My mom had sold the rink out from under me to Ted, her restaurant manager, and after that, she pulled me into her world at Hooligan's. First a job in the restaurant, then renting the space, then bartending, then promotions, and eventually manager. None of it felt accidental. It was like she was trying to funnel me toward something steady after taking away the place I had poured myself into. Though, she never did say those words out loud. Each step looked like progress from the outside, but inside it felt like climbing a ladder that kept changing height depending on her mood or whatever storm she was facing. And when Skip, her husband, was diagnosed with cancer during the free fall of 2008, she told me I had to buy Hooligan's so she could be home with him.

I took it as belief. Maybe even trust. I knew that building. I knew the regulars. I knew exactly what a place like that could be in the right hands. It felt like opportunity, legacy, and challenge all rolled into one, and I've never been great at walking past a challenge. So I said yes. But a part of me shaped by everything that came before already sensed there might be a catch tucked somewhere beneath the offer.

On paper, it sounded doable. Hooligan's would hum along. The lodge would feed the restaurant, the restaurant would feed the bar, and I would thread it all together the way I always had—hard work, creativity, a little bit of showmanship, and a lot of late nights. I told myself I was building something solid for my family, stacking one more layer onto a life that was finally starting to feel stable.

But "one more thing" has a way of multiplying. Days started earlier. Nights stretched longer. I bounced between the restaurant and the bar and the lodge and home like I was on a relay team with no one to pass the baton to. One more delivery. One more staff issue. One more late check-in. I kept saying yes, kept adding, kept convincing myself it was all part of the plan.

For a while, my body moved like it belonged to someone else. Someone who could run a bar, a restaurant, and a 33-room lodge without blinking. I poured drinks, flipped linen schedules, unclogged toilets, and spun dinner specials into poetry, all without leaving the same square mile of small-town Alaska. My hands stayed busy, my feet were always sore, and my brain raced half a beat ahead of the next thing breaking. Inside, an old signal started humming again, low and persistent. I knew that feeling. It was the body's way of tapping the glass, reminding me that even momentum has limits.

Everything that followed didn't unfold in one clean arc. It came in phases—chapters inside the chapter—each one shifting the way I moved through the world. There was the part where the bar demanded more than I had to give. The part where my body threw up a white flag I couldn't ignore. And the part where everything I thought I understood about healing, faith, and second chances cracked wide open. Looking back, it's the only way to make sense of it: the Bar, the Battle, and the Breakthrough. Three currents running through the same river, pulling me under, washing me clean, and spinning me somewhere I never expected to land.

Here's how it all came undone and how it all began again.

PART 1: THE BAR, "THE TAP KEPT FLOWING, BUT I WAS RUNNING DRY"

At first, the sounds were familiar. Glasses clinking, door chimes ringing, laughter folding into jukebox static. But underneath all that, there was something else—a quieter frequency that didn't belong to the bar or the kitchen or the late-night shuffle of regulars. It belonged to me. A kind of internal hum, steady and tired, that started to rise with the type of strength that shows up quietly and doesn't let go, just loud enough to hear.

Running Hooligan's meant more than pouring drinks or tweaking the menu. It meant fielding people's moods, stories, and late-night confessions while keeping your own world in motion. It was about fixing what broke, smoothing over what didn't quite work, and somehow making it all feel effortless. The goal was always to make the place feel like home. Maybe a bit worn in, perhaps a little sticky, but comfortable, like your favorite hoodie. And for a while, it did. But the long hours and constant demands started to chip away until the thing you once loved began to feel like it was running you instead.

Theft hummed in the background, as subtle and constant as a refrigerator hum, until the day it spoiled everything. Inventory didn't just vanish; my faith in people did, too, the kind you can't recover with a refund or a restock.

Still, I poured into them. Maybe it was stubbornness, blind faith, or just a refusal to accept reality, but I clung to the belief that if you gave people a ladder, they'd climb, never imagining they'd set the thing on fire and toast marshmallows over the flames. I treated them like family, hoping they'd rise to meet that trust. I even invited some of them to the big bar and restaurant expo in Vegas: food, hotels, conference passes, the works. I believed in them. I hoped they'd believe in the vision.

For a brief stretch, it actually seemed like we were onto something. We came back from that trip scribbling ideas on napkins, caffeinated and electric, filled with fresh ambition and the kind of sleep-deprived confidence only a hotel conference center can inspire. I was tired, constantly tired, but for the first time in months, I let myself believe we were building something better.

But underneath that excitement, the same theft that had been simmering all along was still happening—and getting bolder.

It didn't all come crashing down in a single headline-worthy implosion. It was quieter than that, more sinister. The unraveling came through late-night calculations that didn't compute, registers that wouldn't square, and a tightening in my chest I tried to explain away as stress. Sleep became a myth. My thoughts were like caffeinated squirrels: chaotic, tireless, gnawing through every corner of my mind. My money was disappearing, my fuse was shot, and every morning I still had to show up and smile like the fries were hot and nothing was on fire.

But even in the rot, some people glittered, like Sarah. She showed up looking for work, jittery as a moth near a bug zapper, eyes darting just a second too fast. I missed the signs at first. By the time I figured out she was on meth, she was already in rotation. I didn't shame her or throw a fit. I just pulled her aside and gave her a choice: Get clean or get gone. No lecture. No spotlight. Just a fork in the road. And she took it. Rehab. Recovery. A baby. A baptism. Now she's years sober and still in touch. Her story reminds me that not all broken things stay broken.

My daughters stepped in, too, showing up like reinforcements in a war I hadn't realized I was losing. At one point, all of us lived in the lodge while our house was under construction. It felt like camping, if your campsite came with deep fryers, shift rosters, and a never-ending to-do list. Wake up, prep, serve, scrub, collapse. Rinse and repeat. Life and work no longer ran in two lanes; they merged into a single, crowded freeway. Through it all, Emerald found her own spotlight: She opened for Hobo Jim with her guitar and sang alongside him for two summers, her voice carrying into the same space that had so often carried me.

Anni, just 16, ran the kitchen like a conductor with a spatula. Orders flew, staff flaked, appliances acted up, and she handled it all with the kind of calm that never asked for credit. She kept things moving, kept people in line, and never once made it about herself. No dramatics, no fuss, just a teenager running a professional kitchen like she'd been doing it her whole life.

That same summer, Hooligan's found its rhythm. The place pulsed with an energy that felt grounded and alive, largely thanks to Hobo Jim. He played Thursday through Saturday, year after year, and his shows turned the bar into a destination. People reserved tables weeks in advance. By the time the lights dimmed and he stepped up to the mic, the room was already full.

They came from all over. Some were locals who never missed a set, some were tourists who stumbled in on stories, and others were well-known names who quietly flew north just to hear him play in that wood-paneled room that smelled like beer and memory. Hobo didn't just perform. He transformed the space. His voice, his presence, the way he carried a room without effort, made the bar feel less like a business and more like a place people belonged to.

After I left Hooligan's, his loyalty never wavered. The new owners called him in, proud to unveil a custom-carved sign that read "The Home of Hobo Jim." He stood there, listened, and told them clearly that after what they did to me, he wanted nothing to do with the place. Then he turned and left. Not because he was angry, but because he meant every word.

But even when the bar was full and the music made the walls vibrate, the strain never really let up. The bright moments helped, but they couldn't cancel out the weight I was carrying behind the scenes. And yet, even with Anni's grit and Lily's redemption, some burdens don't lighten no matter how many hands lift them. Because the heaviest blow didn't come from behind the bar or across the street. It came from home.

When a stranger betrays you, the pain stings in a way that makes sense; it fits into the expected narrative of risk and disappointment. But when the betrayal comes from your mother, it doesn't just hurt; it unravels your sense of direction, distorting your emotional compass in ways that are hard to explain. There is no manual for that kind of loss, no cushion to soften it, no script that prepares you for the silence that follows. What I was losing wasn't only financial stability; I was losing the story I had been telling myself for years, the fragile belief that perhaps, at long last, we were finally creating something together.

My relationship with my mom was always laced with asterisks, love with footnotes. So when she offered to sell me the bar through an owner-financed deal, I let hope tiptoe in. Maybe this was her way of starting fresh. Maybe this was her version of an apology.

But two years in, she showed up out of nowhere and said, "Ted, the guy who bought Sal's, wants Hooligan's. He's offering me $50,000 down. You have three weeks to match it or I'm selling." This was the same guy who had taken the roller rink from me. The memory flickered like old neon, blinking and impossible to ignore.

I didn't have $50,000 lying around in a vault. I sold jewelry, begged lenders, and took out a merchant cash advance, the financial equivalent of bloodletting. My husband didn't understand why I was willing to go to such extremes, but I did. I knew what losing it would mean. I matched the offer, barely, and when my mom didn't hand it over to the other guy, I breathed what felt like my first full breath in months. As far as I knew, the bar was finally mine. The papers weren't perfect, and the building was still in her name, but I believed we had crossed a threshold. I believed the threat had passed.

That loan drained $500 a day straight from our credit card sales. It didn't matter if it was a slow Tuesday or a record-breaking Friday. Every morning, the money disappeared before I even opened the doors. It took $75,000 to pay off that original $50,000. And just when I thought I might finally be on solid ground, I made another big decision.

That trip to the nightclub expo in Vegas, the one I'd taken with my team months earlier, had lit a fuse in me. Everyone was upgrading. New lighting, new menus, new energy. I didn't want to fall behind. So I took out a second loan for $100,000 and poured it into the space. Copper countertops. Polished metal finishes. Trendy barstools that looked like they belonged on the cover of a hospitality magazine. I wanted people to walk in and feel impressed. I wanted them to see a future there.

But I misread the town. They didn't want sleek. They wanted stories soaked into the woodwork. They wanted comfort, not polish. And the kicker? The building was still in my mother's name. She asked for the receipts, saying it was for taxes. I handed them over, not realizing she planned to claim them as deductions.

I took the risk. I paid the price. I gave the place everything I had. She got the write-off. I got the bill. What had once felt like a lifeline, a second chance wrapped in drywall and deep fryers, turned into something else. It became a heavy, silent reminder that not all "inheritances" come with love attached.

The tap kept flowing. But I was the one pouring from an empty glass, hoping no one would notice it was mostly foam.

PART 2: THE BATTLE

That bar didn't just drain my bank account. It siphoned off my trust, my nerve endings, my capacity for small talk, and it pushed the parts of me that were already straining to keep things in focus. For more than 10 years, I'd been shuttling in and out of the neuro-ophthalmologist's office every six months. Each visit meant another round of field tests, another scan, another prescription that needed adjusting. My vision kept shifting in small but noticeable ways, the kind you learn to track because they slowly reshape how you move through the world. I kept moving through work and home and all the in-between spaces, pretending I could keep pace with a body that demanded more effort than I had to give.

When I sat down in her office that day, she glanced up from her computer and delivered the news in the same tone someone might use to mention a chance of rain: "You have about six months left before you're completely blind." Casual. Efficient. Catastrophic.

My head throbbed, my eyes felt strained, and looking straight ahead had become something I had to negotiate rather than assume. The room buzzed in that familiar, fluorescent hum reserved for bad news and sterile spaces.

I wasn't shocked. Not exactly. It just felt like the latest plot twist in a story that had already taken several sideways turns. My vision had been slipping for months, sneaking out the side door while I was busy putting out figurative fires with a wet bar rag. It wasn't surprising, but it still landed with that quiet finality of a favorite song cutting off mid-chorus.

And the truth was, things at home had already been cracking. My marriage to Aaron was wearing thin, stretched out by long silences and a distance that kept growing no matter how much I tried to ignore it. We were still under the same roof, still doing the day-to-day, but the connection had been fading for a while.

Work didn't give me any room to breathe either. It was a nonstop loop of effort without recovery, and I dragged that kind of exhaustion through the door every night. Home, instead of being a place to land, felt like a quiet museum of avoidance—tidy on the outside, hollow underneath. Everything was friction and fog, and I just kept moving through it, bracing myself with caffeine and the kind of grit my family passes down like a birthright.

I didn't broadcast any of it. I've always been pretty good at making functional look easy. But under the surface, I was tired. Not the kind of tired you fix with a nap, but the kind that hums under your ribs and makes everything—thoughts, decisions, basic decency—just a little harder to access. I missed the groundedness I used to feel, the quiet moments where the world softened enough to let something deeper settle in. Church had once been a container for that stillness, but I had stepped away after my family splintered and the rituals began to feel more like obligations than invitations. At the time, it felt like freedom. But somewhere along the way, I realized I had forfeited more than Sunday mornings. I had lost a connection to the mystery, to beauty, to breath.

That longing tapped on the glass again in the most ordinary places. The smell of weathered wood. A certain progression of chords. Afternoon light slanting just so across the floor. Nothing loud. Nothing urgent. Just a thread pulling me gently toward something I couldn't quite name.

Instead of returning to pews and pulpits, I wandered sideways. While juggling the unpredictable demands of a business and a life, I reached for anything that sparked curiosity or calm. Reiki. Tarot. Candles. Crystals. I wasn't staging a performance, and I certainly wasn't being ironic. I built meaning with whatever tools I could find in the spiritual junk drawer.

My daughters came along for the ride, openhearted and curious. We lit candles with intention, rearranged rooms like sacred geometry students, and whispered truths in the kind of hush reserved for bedtime stories and answered prayers. For a while, it gave us something to hold on to, a rhythm and a shared language for wonder that threaded through the day-to-day with just enough grace to keep us steady.

Then the lights flickered. The television turned itself on and off, choosing shows like it had opinions. Shadows behaved with more confidence than they should have. And I, ever the pragmatist with a punch line, met the strange phenomena with a raised eyebrow and a dry remark: If you are going to haunt the house, at least respect the remote. Humor, after all, is my favorite line of defense.

The migraines returned with theatrical flair, sweeping in unannounced and overstaying their welcome. I showed up in the ER so often the nurses and I were on a first-name basis, and the IVs dripped as routinely as coffee. It became background noise, part of the cost of keeping it all together.

Then came that appointment. The chair. The scan. The sentence drifted into the room with the weight of a balloon full of bricks, deceptively light and quietly devastating.

I didn't weep or rant. I just sat there, quiet and motionless, like someone rewatching a slow-motion replay of a moment they already knew was headed off the rails.

In the stillness that followed, with the diagnosis hanging in the air and everything familiar feeling slightly out of place, I finally heard it. There was no voice, no thunder.

Just a stillness that pressed in with quiet insistence, carrying a truth that had been patiently waiting for me to stop pretending.

Something had to change, because even before the darkness made itself official, there had been signs. Subtle flickers at the edge of everything. A light that didn't go out all at once, but stuttered, hesitant, warning, almost tender in its unraveling as if the universe was offering one last shimmer before pulling the room to black.

PART 3: THE BREAKTHROUGH

When the neurologist told me I had six months before I would go blind, I didn't cry, collapse, or scream at the universe. I just sat there, very still, as if my bones were debating whether to keep holding me upright. The words floated around the room, impossible to absorb. It wasn't that I didn't hear them; I just couldn't attach them to the life I was still living. My kids were out there in the world, racing dirt bikes, singing harmonies, scribbling stories, and I was supposed to plan for a future where I couldn't even see their faces?

I walked out of the office with dilated pupils and even

wider thoughts. My vision was blurry, but my disorientation wasn't just physical. I kept bumping into edges, not just of furniture, but of meaning. And instead of calling my husband, my best friend, or even another doctor, I called Sherry Morris.

Sherry wasn't someone close. She was the sister of someone I vaguely remembered from high school. A pastor. A person whose path had crossed mine just enough times that her name had managed to stick. She had once invited me to church in a grocery store aisle. I laughed it off then. Politely, I thought. Maybe a little smugly. After all, I was the woman running the bar with the feather boas and the Fireball shots. I was the woman behind the calendar giveaways, the themed nights, the no-apologies kind of charm. And Sherry never flinched. She didn't guilt, press, or promise me anything. She just kept showing up when I least expected it, as if grace knew where I lived.

And so, when things started to unravel, I said yes. Not in some thunderclap moment of conviction, but more like a sigh of surrender. I told my daughters we were going to church, and we walked in like tourists in our own town, wondering if the pews might squeak their disapproval.

But they didn't. No one turned to gawk. There was no whispered judgment, no side-eyed glances, just warmth.

Disarming, unbothered warmth. And then the music started.

It wasn't the notes themselves that undid me. It was the way they crept in without asking permission. Something in me cracked, not dramatically, but deeply, like a quiet shift beneath the floorboards. I wept. Right there, beside my daughters, mascara betraying me in public. And still, I went back the next week. The tears returned, too, like faithful guests. Something was happening. Not just unraveling. Not just collapse. Something quieter and stranger, like being rebuilt from the inside.

When I called Sherry, sheepish and snotty, to tell her I had cried through another service, she didn't laugh or hand me a pamphlet. She simply said, "That's God cleansing your heart." I didn't know what to do with those words, but they landed with the kind of thud that says, "You might not understand this yet, but you will."

And then came the moment I never expected. When the pastor offered the invitation—If you want to give your life to Jesus, come forward—I didn't debate it. I stood. I walked past the familiar faces, past the quiet knowledge of who I had been and what I had built, and I knelt. Not for show. Not for drama. Just because something had shifted clearly. I didn't care who was watching.

I wept again. This time, not because I was breaking. But because something was lifting. I stayed at the front long after the music faded, while strangers whispered prayers over me like soft cloth over a bruise. Someone asked if I was okay. I said the only thing that made sense: "I've just been through so much." And they nodded. They didn't need the details.

Still, there was no magical curtain drop, no soundtrack swelling in the background. I went back to work. The bar still needed tending. Bills still needed paying. Two nights later, I was standing behind the counter, checking receipts and fielding orders, mascara waterproof for good reason. I was different, but not visibly so. It was a strange limbo, like walking with one foot in warm water and the other on cold tile.

I'd begun to wonder if the light I'd felt had only been passing through when the phone rang. It was the neurologist's office calling with my latest scan results. They asked me to come in for a follow-up. I'd sat through enough of those appointments to know what that usually meant—another scan, another prescription, another round of waiting. But when I met with the doctor, he pulled up the image and paused. He looked at the screen, then at me, then back again, as if the math wasn't adding up.

"Have you done anything different recently?" he asked.

"Well," I said, blinking at the overhead lights, "someone prayed for me last week."

He motioned me over and pulled up the image. "This was your last scan," he said, pointing to the smudge. "And this is today's."

The smudge was gone.

"You don't have this disease anymore," he said. "Your optic nerves are clear. Your pressure is normal. You're . . . fine. You don't have the disease anymore, and you don't even need glasses."

I walked out of that clinic blinking in the daylight. Not because it hurt, but because everything looked new. My daughters were waiting in the lobby, scrolling through their phones like it was any other day. I looked at them, grinning like a woman who'd misplaced her fear. And I yelled.

"I'm healed. Jesus healed me!"

Naturally, they looked horrified. No teenage ego can withstand a mother proclaiming divine healing in a crowded waiting room, as if it were the closing number of a Broadway revival. Their eyes widened, their shoulders tightened, and every silent prayer they'd ever uttered for normalcy vanished into thin air. But I didn't care, not even a little. Something had shifted too deeply for decorum to rein it back in.

I started dialing. It wasn't out of obligation. It came from a fullness that couldn't be contained. I called the ones who had seen me folded over in emergency rooms, the ones who had held my hand when I couldn't hold a thought. The friends who had carried grocery bags, whispered prayers, and watched me squint at birthday candles, traffic lights, and menus I could no longer read. I told them all, with a steadiness I hadn't known I was capable of, that it was gone. The disease was gone. Not just improved or manageable. Absent. And I didn't even need the glasses anymore.

And somehow, the miracle held. It didn't feel like a glitch in the matrix or a medical anomaly waiting to unravel. It settled in the way the sky accepts morning—quietly, consistently, and without debate. The migraines that once arrived like sirens never came back. The dark pressure haunting the corners of my vision melted away and left no echo. What had once been chronic became memory.

I do still wear drugstore readers, of course. Time insists on leaving its fingerprints. But the fear that once claimed so much real estate in my body and my mind is gone. There's no shadow behind my eyes. No ache waiting in the wings.

I remember the slow erosion of hope, the way it receded

so quietly you barely noticed until you were ankle-deep in despair. I remember the constant bracing, the resignation that posed as strength. And I remember, just as clearly, how quickly hope returned. Like a breath you didn't realize you were holding, finally released into the air.

Jesus didn't just take the illness; He lifted the low-grade tension that had threaded itself through my mind and body for years, the kind of unease that grows so familiar you forget what life felt like without it. He didn't come with explanations or demands. His presence settled slowly, like warmth returning to a place gone cold. And as that tension gave way, something in me shifted, not just physically, but in the way I perceived everything around me.

And now, I see differently, not just with healed eyes, but with a vision that extends somewhere deeper.

Chapter 6

THE COOKIE CRUMBLES, AND THEN YOU BAKE ANOTHER BATCH

I didn't plan to walk away from the business I built, but somewhere along the way, having a plan stopped mattering. What began as a dream I had willed into existence through hustle and blind hope—the bar, the restaurant, the lodge—started rotting from within. I wasn't just broke. I was broken. After the struggles with my mom and after surrendering my life to Christ, I realized I could no longer pretend any of it was mine to carry. The weight became unbearable, and the illusion of ownership dissolved the moment my spirit left the building, even if my name stayed on the paperwork.

The signs came subtly. The beer taps still ran, the fryer still hissed and popped, but the pulse of the place had vanished. That Friday-night buzz went silent. What used to smell like excitement and indulgence had turned stale. I stopped showing up with anything close to enthusiasm, and when I did, I moved through the rooms like a ghost caught in the echo of her own past.

And then, almost as if God had been waiting for my quiet detachment to cross some unseen threshold, the unraveling began. It didn't come with fanfare or crisis, but with a series of subtle shifts that, at first, I tried to dismiss as unrelated. In hindsight, it's clear they were anything but. One of my longest-standing employees, someone who had once moved through the business with the kind of trust that doesn't require second thoughts, opened a new bar 12 miles away. It wasn't just that she left, or even that she started something new; it was the uncanny familiarity of what she built. The concept, the atmosphere, even the cadence of events felt eerily familiar. Karaoke nights mirrored my own, the flyers bore language I had written, and the entire brand carried an echo of what I had spent years curating.

At the time, I allowed myself to believe that this might be the hardest part, the rupture I would learn to forgive, the challenge that would test me, but ultimately pass. I thought I could recover, recalibrate, and even offer grace from a distance. But what I had mistaken for a singular betrayal was, in truth, only the first quiet signal of a deeper unraveling. Soon after, another bar opened directly across the street, not miles away but steps, slicing into an already limited stream of patrons and diluting what had once felt like a sure thing. The business didn't collapse overnight. It eroded, one imitation, one divided crowd, one muted Friday night at a time.

This wasn't some glittering metropolis with endless foot traffic and a bottomless appetite for nightlife. It was a small Alaskan town of roughly 3,000, and on a good weekend, maybe 150 felt like drinking in public. Two hundred, if there was karaoke and someone's ex wasn't working the door. When I was the only show in town, people came without hesitation. We had lines that stretched out the door like gossip on payday. The place didn't just serve drinks. It pulsed. It breathed. It had a heartbeat.

As new bars sprouted up like mushrooms after a warm rain, the same modest crowd began to splinter. The party didn't grow. It fractured. Regulars got passed around like a shared pack of cigarettes, and the spark that used to set the room on fire began to flicker. Packed nights thinned to scattered tables and a silence louder than a jukebox on mute. It wasn't water that killed the flame. It was indifference.

The money was one thing. Watching the revenue trickle into a dry creek bed where there used to be a river hurt in all the predictable ways. But the real pain came from something quieter. It was the slow, invisible erasure of identity. Every time I came up with something fresh, a clever promotion, a themed night, or a onetime special that made people laugh or lean in, it would reappear days later, nearly word for word, on another business's feed. They didn't compete; they copied. It wasn't inspiration; it was cannibalism.

And while my ideas were being served up at other bars like reheated leftovers, no credit given, and not even a nod to the original recipe, I was back at the source, trying to cover a tab I never fully agreed to. Most of the debt didn't come from recklessness or poor business instincts. It came from years of blurred lines—emotional, financial, and legal—woven through the kind of family dynamics you don't untangle cleanly. After my mother and I took a time-out, I stepped in to keep the bar from being sold out from under us, signing loan documents that made sense in the moment, even if they didn't reflect the reality of who owned what. I poured money into renovations I couldn't legally claim, trusting history to hold things in place where paperwork didn't. But history can't be notarized. The weight of joint decisions that became separate, and then became no one's, landed on me. I shared the whole story back in chapter 5, and there's no need to relive every detail here, But what followed me into this season wasn't just the emotional bruising of a broken relationship. It was the sharp, daily burden of loan payments and legal gray zones, the kind that leave your name on everything and your peace on nothing.

Just as I was trying to find a rhythm again, the gossip crawled through town like a raccoon rifling my life's trash. You hear it skitter behind closed doors, claws tapping on kitchen tiles, noses wrinkling in judgment. There was nothing elegant or whispered about it, just the greasy thump of someone else's narrative slipping into your story, curling its way through town like smoke under a locked door. In communities like ours, rumors outrun reason. People didn't see the mounting debt I was managing. They didn't see the theft that had been bleeding my business dry behind the scenes. They didn't witness the nights I cried alone in the storeroom or the mornings I walked through the front doors numb and hollow. They only saw what they thought was failure and filled in the rest. I kept trying to outrun the noise, hoping that if I just kept moving, something might eventually settle. But the truth was already shifting beneath my feet.

And then life really pulled the rug out . . . My mom had a stroke. I found her myself and drove her straight to the ER, where a doctor she'd seen many times before told me she couldn't be discharged unless I placed her in assisted living. I nodded like someone who had money and time, even though I had neither. My brothers were all tied up, and while I still had kids at home, it didn't matter; no one was available to help—except my big brother Jay. He was a busy business owner, but he still managed to help me as much as he could. Together, we toured assisted living homes one after another until we finally found a place for her.

As if my mother's condition and the business crisis weren't enough, my daughters' health turned into a mystery no one could solve. One was nearly passing out at school with blood pressure so low it could have doubled as a limbo score. The other was vomiting almost every morning for what felt like weeks. Doctors ran test after test, offering only vague theories, until both girls were eventually diagnosed with a form of fibromyalgia.

Sometimes, when it feels like everything that could go wrong already has, you start bracing for the next hit before it even comes. I remember thinking, *Surely this is the bottom.* Surely nothing else could unravel. But life wasn't done humbling me. It was as if God was asking, *Are you still holding on? Let's see about that.* I had no idea how many more pieces would fall, or how close I was to something that would finally break me open.

And just when I thought I had nothing left to give, my body called it. I had a stroke, technically a TIA (transient ischemic attack), but there was nothing minor about the way it short-circuited me. It felt like my brain had been yanked out of gear and jammed back in without checking the clutch. But even then, I didn't stop. I was too afraid of what might collapse if I did. So I did the next thing that made sense at the time: I hired help.

Through a classified ad.

Which, in hindsight, is like hiring a pilot off a bathroom wall because they wrote "trust me" in Sharpie. The guy said he was a bar-world savant, part mixologist, part manager, part savior. I checked his references. They rang with choirboy enthusiasm. For one brief, glimmering second, I thought I'd finally caught a break.

So I handed him the keys, both literal and symbolic,

and stepped back to recover, while my brain still sputtered like a flickering fluorescent bulb that didn't know if it was coming or going. Within weeks, he siphoned thousands of dollars like a Vegas magician but without the tuxedo or the decency. He slid into the staff, slithered behind the bar, and spread chaos like it was cream cheese on a toasted everything bagel. He hit on the waitresses with all the charm of a used car salesman trying to sell a lemon as a Cadillac. He was in his late 20s and gave off the kind of energy that made you want to boil your hands after shaking his. Then came the drugs. Not subtle, not soft. Meth and cocaine, like a touring band with too much gear and no concept of volume control. He brought them in, used them, and got others hooked. Before long, the bar stopped being a bar and became a petri dish.

I fired him. But by then, the rot had spread beyond the bar and into my home. Both my girls smoked pot in the house (we were told it would help with their fibromyalgia), which torpedoed a marriage already sagging in the middle. My husband, a juvenile probation officer, walked in from work to find the air thick with the scent of weed. It was like living inside an awkward anti-drug commercial. I don't know how I made it through that stretch. I was broke and overrun, carrying the whole mess like a waitress with too many plates and no busboy in sight. My husband packed up his patience and left. My daughters scattered like bright birds before a storm. One enrolled in the Job Corps to escape the wreckage. The other begged to move in with a friend, keeping a countdown on her phone for the day she turned 18. Months before that date, I didn't have any fire left in me, so I told her to go.

And so it was just me and my son. Alone. In a building that used to hum with life like a jukebox on a Saturday night, now quiet as the inside of a drained aquarium, glass walls intact but everything vibrant gone. The business still stood, shaped like something alive, but it felt more like a taxidermied version of itself, propped up, hollow, the spirit long gone. My family, the one I had held together with sheer will and whispered prayers, had scattered like confetti at a parade no one showed up for. I was broke, with nothing but a shell of a business and a weight I could no longer carry.

One night, I sank to the sticky floor of the bar. I didn't know what else to do. My back rested against the cooler. My legs gave out in front of me. The room was quiet except for the hum of the fridge and the faint buzz of a neon sign in the window.

I sat there for a long time. Empty. Tired in a way that

went past sleep, and I prayed. Crying, I told God I couldn't carry it anymore. I let go of the business, the pain, the weight of everything I had tried so hard to hold together, right there on the floor that had carried so much of my undoing. I gave it all to Him. I said, "You can have it all. It's Yours."

And then I heard it: a voice. A still, small voice.

Everything you need is here.

I saw it before I touched a single thing: pallet walls, copper pipes, vintage scraps rescued from the shadows. The basement held a hoarder's dream of old stuff, the kind of junk you either haul to the dump or turn into art, depending on how desperate you are. I didn't have money. Not "tight budget" not having money, but "payment plans on the utilities, bar closed, and five employees camped out at the lodge" not having money. Still, I had imagination, and I had a pulse, which in my book was enough to start.

I went to my dad's pawnshop and checked out a staple gun, a drill, and a skill saw. Three tools I didn't know how to use, but figured I'd learn before I lost any more daylight. I dropped my son off at school each morning, then headed to the bar. Not to open it, not to drink, but to tear it apart and rebuild it from the bones. I saved every screw I could pull from the walls. I dismantled pallets like they were treasure chests, hoarding nails like gold coins. I painted the walls black, mounted scavenged copper piping, made a bench out of an old mattress wrapped in bank bags, those old heavy ones made of that canvasy julep stuff, and crowned it with a pallet wall. I even dug up a fishing pole and hung it on the wall because this was a fishing town, and that kind of thing mattered here. I strung oars from the ceiling on bits of rope, then later hung the entire boat they came in from the rafters. Not alone, though. That part came after Jennifer.

One day, in the middle of all the sawdust and scrap piles, a woman walked in. She looked about 10, maybe 15, years older than me, hair pulled back, eyes sharp but kind. She glanced around like she'd stepped into a tornado made of lumber and nails.

"Sweetie," she said, "what are you doing? I came in to have lunch . . . What's going on here?"

I was crouched on the floor with a copper pipe in one hand and a staple gun in the other.

"Oh," I said, wiping my cheek with the back of my hand. "I'm remodeling."

She looked around again. "Who's helping you?"

I stood up and shrugged. "No one. It's just me . . . Just me."

She tilted her head. "How can you do this by yourself?"

I smiled, but only with my mouth. "Well, I'm hoping I'll get it done by summer. Tourist season."

She nodded slowly. "Sweetie, you need help."

I said, "Well, I can't afford help."

And that was it. She gave me one last look, then turned and left. I went right back to work.

The next morning, she came back. This time, she was carrying a box of muffins and cookies in her arms, with eight strangers following behind her like a calm, determined army.

I blinked. "What's this?"

She smiled. "This is for the people who showed up."

I looked at her. "What do you mean?"

"I asked around to see if anyone would help you if I provided snacks. They said yes."

They came back every day for a full week. No permission slips. No drama. Just a quiet parade of capable hands and kind hearts. They worked until the place started looking less like a disaster zone and more like a dream with muscle behind it.

I couldn't tell you their names if you asked me now. They didn't wear name tags or glide in with any fanfare. But it felt like my place was suddenly packed with angels. The kind that wear flannel and work boots and smell faintly of sawdust and coffee cake. They didn't ask a lot of questions. They just glanced around like celestial contractors on a tight schedule and said, "What do you need done?"

I pointed here and there. "This here, that over there." And they moved, fluid as honey on a warm biscuit. One started sanding the bar with the focus of a monk in a woodshop. Another cleaned up broken boards like he was defusing landmines. A few of them hauled that boat up into the rafters like it was the Ark itself, delivered right on time. I bought pizza when I could. Jennifer brought the muffins and cookies that started it all.

And right in the middle of it, like God was tossing in a bonus round, I got a phone call from one of the nicer hotels in town. The kind with the lobby fireplace and fresh fruit water by the elevator. Meanwhile, I was running a lodge with 33 rooms and mattresses that could file assault charges. The hotel manager said, "We're required to replace all our beds every two years, even the barely used ones. Would you like some of them for your place?" I nearly dropped the phone.

I rented a U-Haul for $19.95. The muffin-fed miracle crew and I loaded that thing again and again. We swapped out every spring-poked, lumpy mattress at the lodge for pillow tops that still smelled like lemony detergent and corporate overkill. I didn't have time or money to take the old ones to the dump, so I posted on Facebook: **Free beds. Come get one.** And people did. All day long, they came and hauled them away like they were made of gold instead of mystery stains.

I don't know what kind of angelic favor I cashed in, but somehow the right people walked through the door exactly when I needed them. And whatever blessing made that happen, I hope it circles back their way a hundred times over.

Still, rebuilding the physical space was only half the job.

The next step was dismantling the old version of the bar, the culture, the crowd, and the baggage, just as carefully as the furniture. The local bartending scene had become toxic. There was burnout. Gossip. Drugs. Too many hurt feelings and bridges reduced to ash. And I couldn't pretend my hands were clean in all of it. So I made the only choice that felt honest. I started over. Gave it a new name: Hooked Alehouse and Grill. It was a little cheeky, a little heartfelt. We leaned into bold Alaskan flavors, serving local beer and food. I hung fishing rods, nets, and lures on the walls as if they were museum pieces or relics from a different life. This was my reckoning.

That summer, I hired a young man named Michael. He told me he wanted to come work at Hooked, and I asked if he had any friends who might want to join him. He just grinned and said, "Yeah, I've got plenty." Sure enough, he brought six of them. They were young adults in their 20s, fresh from Anchorage, the big city. They had no idea about the small-town drama or the rumors that had been swirling around me for years. They showed up excited, wide-eyed, and beautiful. Some of them had even modeled before, and suddenly, my little upstairs had been turned into a makeshift bunkhouse. I crammed them into three rooms for the summer, and together we were off and running.

They gave me everything they had: steady hands, long hours, and an energy that felt untainted by the mess that had nearly drowned me. Their presence was like fresh air blowing through a house that had been shut up too long. And then, as if to crown the season, Hobo Jim came. His music carried through the walls like it was meant to live there all along. It was the best season Hooligan's, by then reborn as Hooked Alehouse and Grill, had ever seen. We made more money that summer than at any point in the history of the place.

The blessings did not stop there. Paul, a local man, helped me get my liquor license back after the chaos with my mom and the paperwork fiasco had stripped it away. He loaned me $10,000, something I never would have expected. He only did it because Hobo Jim called and asked, saying he needed a stage to play on and wanted to make sure I had one. It felt like help was materializing from places I had stopped even hoping for.

Every night, Emerald sang "The End of the World" while Hobo Jim played beside her. It was a haunting, beautiful duet that marked the quiet handoff between her voice and his. It wasn't meant to open the night with flash or noise. It was more like a ritual, a gentle way to tell the room the music was about to shift. After the final note,

Emerald stepped down from the stage, tied on her apron, and began serving tables. Her sister, Anni, stayed in the kitchen, holding down the line. And Luke, just nine years old, filled sauce and ranch cups or jumped in wherever he was needed, determined to be part of it all.

That summer felt like a return to life. The upstairs rooms were packed with wide-eyed staff from Anchorage. The place was alive again.

Hobo Jim died two years later. The cancer didn't linger or send warnings. It arrived quietly, the way winter comes to Alaska, certain and cold, with no interest in waiting. One day he was onstage, guitar in hand, doing what he had always done. Playing for a full house, filling the room with sound and memory. And not long after, he was gone.

Alaska does not grieve loudly. It does not put sorrow on display. But that week, people lit candles. They played his songs in their cars and on porch radios. And some came back to Hooligan's, because that's where the memories were.

By the end of that summer, the same doctor who had treated my daughters and who had seen me countless times over the years in Soldotna approached me. He asked if I had ever thought about selling the bar, the restaurant, and the hotel. My answer came quickly, almost without breath.

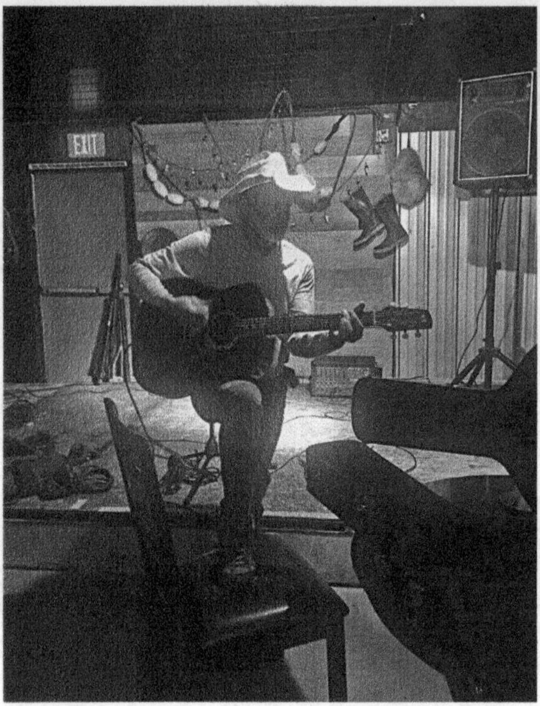

Hobo Jim at Hooligan's—remembered for his music, his kindness, and the steady goodness that defined him.

"Absolutely. I praise God—it's an answer to prayer."

We didn't just leave behind a business. We left with the songs still in our heads and the stories still in our bones. Hobo Jim's music had filled that place once, and no sale could take that away.

ESCROW LIMBO AND THE LAST $150

Escrow. The word has a smug, buttoned-up sound, like it belongs in a banker's hymnbook. On paper, it's supposed to be a neutral vault: the buyer's money on one shelf, the seller's property on another, everything safe until the signatures line up. In theory, it protects both sides. In reality, it's purgatory. You're no longer the owner, but you're not free either. You're dangling in a waiting room where the clock doesn't move and the air grows stale.

I sat in that limbo for nine long months. Nine months of hearing, "We'll close in a few weeks," or "by the end of the month," only to watch the finish line drift further and further out, like a mirage in the desert.

While I waited for the sale to close, the buyers—a wealthy couple—treated me like I already worked for them. They didn't just lean on me; they used every bit of my experience, my connections, my know-how from years of running businesses in this town. I kept my own bar and lodge running and somehow ended up working for them. Midnight calls were constant.

"Come over. We need to talk."

I'd drag my son out of bed in his pajamas, because

leaving him wasn't an option, and sit in their living room while they walked me through their plans for *their* other ventures. It wasn't mentorship or partnership. It was free labor dressed up as "trust."

By daylight, the errands stacked up higher. I was building their websites, sketching their logos, painting their walls, even brainstorming concepts for businesses I wanted nothing to do with. They were expanding their little empire with my hands, my ideas, and my time. And I kept doing it because I needed that sale to go through—because they held the keys to my freedom.

Every time I worked up the nerve to ask about the closing, the wife's voice cracked like a whip: "If you're going to be so difficult, maybe we just won't buy your business."

The longer it went on, the smaller I became. They wore me down until I apologized for things I hadn't done, until I caught myself begging, "Please, just buy my business. I'm sorry."

The days blurred. I was stretched so thin I felt see-through, moving from one demand to the next without ever catching my breath. Nights bled into mornings, mornings into more chores for them. It was like living on a conveyor belt that never slowed, just kept rolling me forward, one more task, one more compromise.

And still, they pressed for more.

Even the holidays offered no reprieve. That New Year's Eve, instead of church, they summoned me to their "wonderful dinner." I arrived hoping, maybe foolishly, for warmth, a break, a reminder of everyday life. Instead, they shoved a pile of crab in front of me and told me to get shucking. Hours later, she peered into the little bowl I'd managed and sneered, "That's all you got out of that crab?"

Their reasons kept mutating.

Finally, nine months in, ten minutes before we were supposed to sign, they called with one last twist. "We can pay off your mom's loan"—a loan I didn't even know existed until we went into escrow—he said, "but we don't have anything left for you. Would you owner-finance the rest?" It was the kind of call that should've set off alarms, but by then I was so wrung out I couldn't tell exhaustion from relief. I should have said no, but I couldn't see another way. I had creditors breathing down my neck, bills stacked like firewood, and the summer tourist season right around the corner. I agreed on a small sum each month and the near same at closing. Even then, they tried to wriggle out of paying that last bit up front. I told them I wouldn't close without it, and they caved, but only because they smelled profit on the horizon.

They had promised me peace. They had promised to pay off everyone I owed. Instead, they shoved that mess back in my lap. I walked away from the table still carrying debt like a stone baby strapped to my chest, and I was the one writing checks I thought were already covered.

At first, I clung to the hope that at least the monthly payments would steady me. But the second month came, April, and nothing showed up. May—still nothing. By June, the silence was deafening. Each time I called, I was met with a new excuse: The bank was slow, the paperwork hadn't cleared, the funds were tied up somewhere else. Excuses piled up like junk mail you don't remember subscribing to.

Meanwhile, I drove past the property and saw a different story. The place was alive with crews and contractors, ladders leaned against the siding, hammers clanging, money flowing like a river I couldn't touch. They were remodeling the building I had poured my life into, and I couldn't even set foot inside.

When I finally tried, their employees looked at me like I was a stranger and told me flat-out: I'd been 86'd. Banished. From my own building. My calls went unanswered.

By then, I was down to my last $150. The building stood in their name. The bills sat in mine. I had a house, a mortgage, a son to feed, and a reputation unraveling fast. To the town, I looked like a fraud. I had spent nine months saying, "We're about to close," and nothing ever happened. Nobody believed I was being strung along. To them, it was just another episode in the never-ending saga of Molly.

But it wasn't drama to me. It was survival. Every day I woke up juggling creditors, bills, and shame, hoping the math would somehow bend in my favor. Instead, it mocked me. The ledger stayed blunt: $150. That was all.

I wasn't just broke. I was humiliated. Stripped of pride, stripped of options, standing at the edge of collapse with nothing but a crumpled handful of bills between me and the void. One hundred and fifty dollars. That was the flimsy thread holding up the weight of my whole world.

Chapter 7

THE BIRTH OF BOOZY COOKIES

(And the Taco Truck That Started It All)

I never planned to become the cookie queen of a taco trailer. The truth is, it all started with a vision. Driving my son up to Eagle River to see his dad, I saw it as clear as day: me on the side of the road, selling halibut tacos. I shook it off as strange, but on the drive back, the vision returned. God has always shown me things like that, so I paid attention.

I thought to myself, *Well, I guess I'm doing this.* With my last $150, I called the food safety office of Alaska. Permits usually crawled like a moose in molasses, but mine zipped through in just two days. I didn't even own proper equipment. My plan was laughably bare-bones: a folding table, a tent, and a couple of buckets that could double as kitchen tools and a makeshift confessional. Still, doors kept swinging open like a row of saloon doors in some cosmic Western. Country Foods, the supplier I already owed money to, handed me a $500 line of credit. The city of Soldotna gave me the green light, but with one twist: no wheels, no tacos. I needed a trailer.

I hit my knees and prayed. "God, You gave me this vision. You've opened every door. Why stall me now?" And then I heard it: *Call Ken.*

Ken was a character from another lifetime, back in my Sassafras days, 20 years earlier. He had been in the trailer business. I called, half-expecting he'd forgotten me. Instead, he said, "I've only got one left. Come look at it." I drove over, bracing for a rusted box I'd have to MacGyver into something barely functional. What he rolled out instead looked like a gift straight from God: a fully equipped food trailer, complete with sink, freezer, fridge, and counters, already blessed by the Alaska Department of Environmental Conservation. It was as if destiny had been shrink-wrapped in aluminum siding. I had no money, but Ken, smiling through his suspenders, simply said, "Borrow it. Six weeks. Pay me later if you can."

My dad hauled it home like a miracle on wheels. I painted a chicken on the side with 79-cent tempera paints and lettered, right there on the metal, "**Save a chicken, eat fish.**" I cut a striped awning from bargain-bin fabric and held it up with duct tape, so it flapped like a carnival flag. That summer, my son, Luke, was 10 years old, old enough to know we were hustling for survival, but still young enough to treat the whole thing like an adventure. He was elbow-deep in five gallons of Craisin-pineapple coleslaw, mixing with the kind of reckless joy only kids possess.

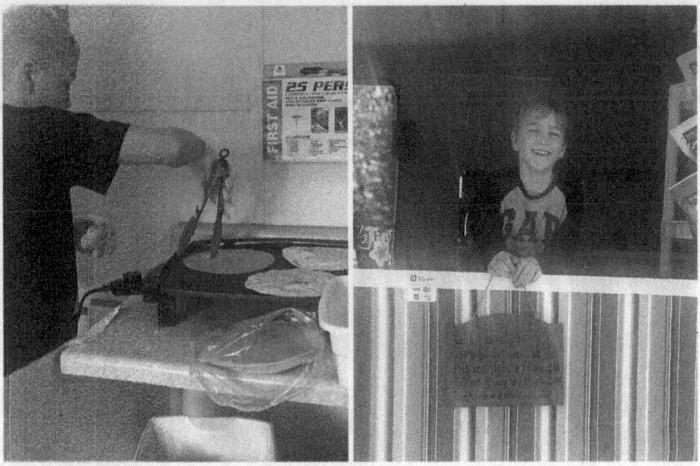

Luke at the family's makeshift fish-taco stand, pitching in with the same joy that kept the little trailer running.

A friend and local pastor, Vickie Walber, loaned me an air fryer that hissed like a miniature space shuttle. My dad brought his generator. I priced the halibut tacos at five dollars apiece and slid open the window. We fell into a rhythm. Grill the fish, wrap the tacos, pass them through the window with a smile and a quiet prayer that tomorrow would be at least as busy as today.

The city had one more rule to keep us on our toes. We were only allowed to keep the trailer parked on-site for three days at a time. Every third night, my dad would hook it up, haul it to my driveway, and back it in. Then, the next morning, he pulled it out again and returned it to the lot. Exhausting, yes, but it forced us to stop, clean, and reset. Those cycles kept the trailer sanitary and gave us just enough breathing room to catch up before the next rush.

The first day, we made $126. The next day, we doubled it. Then doubled it again. By the fourth day, as halibut tacos flew out the window in little paper boats, a customer leaned in and asked, "Do you have anything sweet?"

Luke laughed and said, "You should make cookies." It sounded half like a joke and half like a dare. He knew I burnt cookies all the time, but it stuck. I didn't know much about baking, but I had a credit line with Country Foods, so I asked if they carried premade cookie dough. They did, and that was enough.

My sister-in-law Marta stopped by right then. She had already lent me her garage-sale money box, a serving spoon, and anything else she could spare. In our family, she was the dessert queen, sweet to her core, always ready to help. I handed her the dough and said, "Make cookies. Just do your thing." She made plain chocolate chip cookies, and they were gone by lunch.

The next day, Luke and I tried our hand at tweaking the mix. We dumped in Cocoa Pebbles from the cupboard, and those sold too. But the premade dough was expensive, and I knew if this was going anywhere, we'd have to figure out scratch baking. I flipped over a Nestlé Toll House bag, followed their recipe, and pulled out a tray of cookies that spread into flat, sad pancakes. I dove into research on making them fluffier, tweaking little things until I got closer.

At the same time, I experimented with whatever I had on hand. There was cereal like Cinnamon Toast Crunch, mountains of marshmallows, and enough imagination to turn it into a s'mores cookie. Then I started following hashtags like *#GourmetCookies* on Instagram and collecting ideas from Pinterest. The maple bacon donut was having its moment, so I fried bacon, whipped up maple frosting, a touch of whiskey from the old bar days, and out came the Bossman cookie. It was salty and sweet and a little outrageous. People went crazy for it.

I also had a garage full of leftover liquor from the bar. In Alaska, when you sell a bar, you take the alcohol home. I wasn't really a drinker anymore, but the bottles were there. At first, I poured bourbon or tequila straight into the dough, thinking the alcohol would bake out. It didn't. Later, I learned cookies never reached a high-enough temperature for that. Still, those early "boozy cookies" sold like wildfire. Eventually, I got smarter about it.

One night, scrolling Facebook, I saw a meme: "Vanilla extract is made of vodka. Let's party." It stopped me cold. All that alcohol sat in the garage, practically begging for a purpose. I looked up how to make an extract and learned that you need vanilla beans soaking in vodka for three months. I didn't have three months. Ken wanted his trailer back in five weeks.

Instant Pots had just come out, and I borrowed one from a friend who never used his. I buried myself in YouTube videos and blog posts until I figured it out. In three days, I turned every bottle into an extract—vodka, Kahlua, Baileys, whiskey, Fireball, everything I had. Then I kept going and made bacon extract and herbes de Provence extract. Suddenly, I had flavor without the alcohol and endless possibilities.

That's when the cookies took on a life of their own. I called them *loaded cookies*. I would tell people, "This one has maple, bacon, and whiskey extract," and their eyes lit up. Years in the bar business had taught me how to sell with a name and a smile. Soon, I was cranking out combinations like apricots with macadamia nuts and brandy, bourbon chocolate chip, Kahlua pumpkin spice with cream cheese, whiskey with bacon, and white chocolate and maple. People bought one, then circled back to clear out the whole tray. Before long, we were known as the taco truck with the best cookies.

Meanwhile, life at home was bare-bones but steady. We sold the pictures off our walls, the dining table, and even Luke's bed, so he slept with me. We sold the TV and used a projector against the wall. I even parted with jewelry just to cover the bills. It was embarrassing and humbling, but it stripped away my pride. God was teaching me to see only Him. And if anyone brought up my past from the bar days, I could say, "That was me then, and I have been redeemed."

Most nights, I collapsed into bed after prep, exhausted yet unable to rest. I applied for jobs while also starting to write my book *How to Be Fearless in Business*.

Back at the trailer, the momentum only grew. Soon, there were lines at the window for tacos and cookies, music thumping like our own little block party. One afternoon came the knock I'll never forget. I opened the back door, and there was Celeste, Pastor Vickie's sister, one of the women who had lent me an air fryer at the very beginning. She smiled and said, "I do not care what flavor cookies you have today. I want to buy them all." Behind her, cars were stacked like a drive-through, while the walk-up line stretched in the other direction. Luke and I just stared at each other, wide-eyed, barely keeping up. It was one of those moments that made me want to cry and laugh at the same time. Celeste has since passed away, but her sister, Pastor Vickie, is still here, still amazing.

When summer ended, Ken came for his trailer. He asked if I wanted to buy it, but I couldn't afford to. I had managed to catch up my bills and had about $300 left to my name. So I told him, "No, but I'll sell it for you." He asked $13,000, and I put it on Facebook for $14,000. When it sold, I handed him the $13,000 he wanted and gave him the extra $1,000 as a thank-you for trusting me with his trailer for the summer. He hadn't asked for it, but I wanted him to know how much it meant to me. He was so grateful, and I was too. What a sweet man. "I'll never forget you," I said. And I meant it.

When he drove away, I stood there for a minute, taking in the stillness that followed. The summer had felt like one long stretch of improvising my way through each day, but once the dust settled, I could sense something deeper had been at work. God had been stripping things down, not to harm me, but to rebuild me. What I had just lived through wasn't only about tacos, or trailers, or figuring out how to keep the lights on one more month. It was what I now call my Job season.

In the Bible, Job loses everything yet refuses to cut ties with God. That story is less about suffering and more about the strange persistence of faith. That was me. I lost my bar, my money, my reputation, and, for a while, even family ties. People—even family—told me to declare bankruptcy, to pack it in, to walk away from the mess of it all. But something in me would not let go of the idea that restoration was still possible.

And it came, though not in the form anyone expected.

It arrived as a taco trailer with a crookedly painted chicken, a hair straightener pressed into service as a cookie sealer, and a 10-year-old boy elbow-deep in coleslaw who still thought of it all as an adventure. From scraps and odd tools, a brand began to take shape.

By the time the summer was over, I knew Soldotna couldn't hold what God was building. The season of gravel lots and taco trailers had done its work. With Luke by my side and more faith than money, I packed up and headed for Anchorage—ready to find out what this story would become on a bigger stage.

TO BAKE YOUR DREAMS COME TRUE

Mornings in our house didn't begin with yoga flows or oat milk cappuccinos. They started with the *wrrrrrrr* of a dusty projector warming up against a blank wall, casting cartoons and colors onto the space where a TV used to be. But we didn't mourn the furniture. Somehow, even when the house echoed with the hollowness of missing things, it rang louder with our laughter. Luke and I made magic out of hand-me-down blankets and grocery store popcorn, turning our pared-down space into a campfire of joy. We cuddled, giggled, and played *Mario Kart* like it was a sport that could earn us medals, or at least momentary peace. When church was on, we went. When church was off, we raced Koopa Troopas and thanked God anyway.

Still, nights came when the weight of bills pressed hard. I finally swallowed my pride and went to my church to ask for help. I had only been there a year, and it humbled me to walk through those doors with nothing but a stack of overdue notices in hand. My pastor, Sherry, looked me straight in the eye and said, "Write down all the bills you have." I did, and she paid my phone bill, my gas bill, and covered the rest for that month. I'll never forget it, because everything was about to be shut off. Her generosity kept the lights on, not just in the house, but in my heart. I never had anything disconnected, and I didn't lose my car or our home. God was faithful.

Everything back then felt a little like rummaging

through a junk drawer, hoping something inside would spark an idea or a miracle. One afternoon, while cleaning out my garage to sell whatever I could for gas and grocery money, I found an old stand mixer buried behind a pile of boxes. It felt like more than a discovery; it felt like a gift. A quiet moment of reassurance, like God was saying, "I see you." But it came with a catch–it had no attachments, and I only had $35 in my bank account. I scraped it together and went to the store, praying for a way to make it work. The only attachment in the entire store, the very last one on the shelf, was a cookie paddle. It was sitting there like it was glowing at me, marked at $34. I had just enough. God did this for me again and again, testing my faith to the very last minute. And each time, I chose to be faithful. And each time, so was He.

Days carried on in their own patchwork way after that, ordinary moments stitched with small signs that we weren't forgotten. Every Wednesday, Luke and I attended the church potluck, which guaranteed a solid meal. I remember one week I only had five dollars. We stopped at 7-Eleven, because everyone had to bring something to share. There they were, Hostess powdered donuts, two packs for five bucks. I was embarrassed, but Luke shrugged and said, "Whatever, we'll just do it." We walked in and set the donuts on the counter, and before long, people were asking, "Who brought the powdered donuts? I love those!" I caught the pride glowing on Luke's face. God sees you right where you're at, even when you show up with nothing but sugar-dusted donuts from a gas station.

I refused to let scarcity shape Luke's spirit. We didn't have much, but I didn't want him growing up feeling afraid of lack or defined by it. So, when he asked for something and the numbers didn't make sense, I said no with a steady voice. Not fearful. Not apologetic. Just honest. I wanted him to learn that a no didn't mean we were "less than." It simply meant we were choosing differently. It meant the moment mattered more than the stuff.

Somewhere in the middle of that season, I got inspired by a Kardashian. Not the glamorous ones with makeup lines and Met Gala gowns, but Rob, the brother with a sock subscription service. Most people rolled their eyes at him. I paid attention. If socks could have a fan club, why not cookies? And not just any cookies. I wanted something bolder. Boozy cookies, loud in flavor and branding, full of sass and unapologetic fun. I wanted people to open the box and feel something: surprise, delight, maybe even mischief. That is when the oven box idea came to me. A four-burner stove on top, a flap that opened like an oven door, and, nestled inside, cookies that looked like they just slid out of a bakery dream. Right on the lip of the box, in small print but big spirit, I stamped the phrase: "To bake your dreams crumb true."

That little idea grew legs fast. I stumbled across a platform called Cratejoy while watching *Ellen* one day, and I signed up before the episode was even over. Loaded Cookies was officially born: a cookie-of-the-month club featuring rotating flavors, boozy extracts, and all the flair I could pack into a dozen.

I started small. Orders came through Facebook posts where I would ask things like, "Who's got a birthday coming up? Who needs cookies this week?" Most weeks, I was doing 20 boxes, mostly locals, with some Cratejoy orders. The Cratejoy ones cost me, honestly. I was paying shipping out of pocket, which meant those sales were not padding my bank account. They were draining it. But I knew I had to start somewhere.

Every dozen I sold gave me just enough to buy more butter, flour, sugar, and chocolate. I was making a dollar a cookie. If I sold 10 boxes, that was $120 to survive on. It was not covering my mortgage. But it bought groceries. Paid one utility bill. It let me keep going.

I had three decades in the restaurant industry. I had

owned a successful bar for nine years. Still, I could not land a job, not even at Panda Express. So I baked cookies all night and applied for jobs all day. We made do with what was left.

A coffee shop in Wasilla reached out. They wanted to try the cookies, which meant a five-hour drive across snowy Alaskan roads to deliver a single box of 18. I didn't make a penny, but when they reordered, I drove the route again. Still, there was no profit, but it was my pastor's daughter's shop, and her belief in me carried more weight than any margin.

Then came Luke's birthday—September 25. He turned 11, and I had nothing in my account, not even gas money or a grocery buffer. My dad gave Luke $20 for his birthday, and Luke asked if we could get a Happy Meal. I smiled and said yes, then gently asked if we could use his birthday money to buy it. That moment split me. I didn't let him see it, but inside I broke open. That night, after he fell asleep, I made a promise to myself in the dark: I would never be this broke again. Not for me. Not for Luke.

The orders were still coming in slowly, sometimes one or two a day, occasionally five. But then, one December morning, I opened my email inbox and nearly dropped my coffee. Forty-five orders had landed overnight. I refreshed the page twice just to be sure. Turns out, BuzzFeed had featured Loaded Cookies as one of the top boozy gift boxes of the year. We were ranked number 3 out of 24, right up there with curated cocktail kits and wine subscriptions. I hadn't submitted anything. They found me on their own. That little mention lit a match under everything I'd been trying to build.

I picked up the phone and called Pastor Vickie, whose church had a commercial kitchen. "I just got an order for forty-five dozen cookies," I said. "They're due tomorrow. Can I use your kitchen?" She didn't miss a beat. "Come over," she said. When I arrived, I stepped into what felt like a sugar-splashed miracle. Five convection ovens, a 30-quart mixer the size of a toddler, and shelves stocked with flour, butter, and eggs. All of it donated, all of it open to me. She pointed to a whiteboard and said, "Write down whatever you use. I'll check it every morning and restock."

She didn't blink when I told her the cookies were boozy. She didn't judge. She believed. That kind of belief doesn't show up in your ledger, but it's the oxygen that keeps you going when you're gasping for momentum.

Luke skipped school that day to help. We baked, packaged, labeled, and stacked those cookies like elves on a Christmas deadline. I didn't even own a printer, so every address was handwritten, each label a blend of ink and determination. The next day brought another 45 orders. And the day after that. Suddenly, we were in a sugarcoated cyclone.

I brought in my best friend, Billie, a former cook I'd met through church, to help me stay afloat. Luke, sweet as he was, eventually asked if he could please go back to school. His arms were tired, his eyes droopy, and he missed recess. I kissed him on the forehead and let him be a kid again while the rest of us kept baking.

As the cookie train gathered steam, other shops started calling. Coffee spots, small grocery stores, and even restaurants wanted to add my cookies to their shelves. Then, out of nowhere, came an invitation to pitch at something called 1 Million Cups. A friend said it was like *Shark Tank*—a place where you could share your business idea and get actual funding. So I baked ten dozen cookies, boxed them with care, built a little slideshow, and drove three hours through the mountains to Anchorage.

When I got there, I learned it wasn't *Shark Tank*. It wasn't even Trout Tank. It was a feedback forum. Just opinions, no investors. I sat there holding back tears, thinking about the money I didn't have, the time I couldn't spare, and the hope that had gotten ahead of the facts.

But in that room, a woman named Whitney approached me. She worked for Brown Jug, a 21-store liquor chain. "We heard about your cookies," she said. "We came to try them. They're amazing. We want to carry them in all our stores. Do you have UPC codes? Nutrition labels?"

I smiled, heart racing. "Absolutely," I said. I had no clue what either of those required.

I drove home, picked up Luke from school, and got to work. After days of searching and making dozens of phone calls, I found a website that offers unlimited nutrition labels for $45 a month. I signed up and figured it out. I bought UPCs. I refashioned my oven boxes with makeshift display facings made from cardboard and tape. I baked all night, dropped Luke off in the morning, drove back to Anchorage with the first official order, and returned just in time for school pickup. Brown Jug sold out in 24 hours.

When I look back now, I see that the real miracle wasn't the cookies or the sales. It was what cracked open inside me. For most of my life, I lived like a one-woman circus act, juggling, sprinting, improvising everything by the seat of my pants. That season forced me to stop white-knuckling and start listening. Scripture says "do not fear" 365 times, one for each day of the year, and I finally began to treat it as instruction instead of ornament. Faith stopped being a word I hung on a wall and became the thing that carried me forward.

And nowhere was that clearer than the night my faith was tested with $800 and a phone bill for $790. It was months behind and a miracle in itself that it had not shut off. For the first time in what felt like forever, I had just enough to cover it. I planned to go to church, then take care of the bill the next morning—but during the offering, I felt that unmistakable tug in my spirit, the kind that defies logic and doesn't translate well on paper. It was a quiet, undeniable sense that God was asking me to give it all, every last dollar. I wrestled with it, fully aware of what would happen if I obeyed. The phone company would shut off my phone, leaving me with no way to contact anyone. But I also recognized His voice. And I'd made a promise long ago that if He ever asked me for everything, I wouldn't hold back. Obedience is greater than sacrifice. So I gave it all, without drawing attention, without needing anyone to understand. That night, I didn't go home with answers. I went home with peace. The peace God promises, peace that surpasses all understanding.

The very next morning, I felt a clear nudge from God. I heard, "Go to Sysco." So I did. I showed up at Sysco, a food distributor that represents major national brands, with nothing but a Tupperware full of cookies and a business card. I hadn't reached out ahead of time, didn't fill out a form, and hadn't scheduled a meeting. I just walked in, believing something would happen. And it did. David, the sales lead, told me he would reach out if they were interested. I emailed him a few days later. No response. Then, a week later, David from Sysco emailed me. That email became the open door that had been completely closed the day before. Their opening order was $7,000. My biggest deal yet by seven times.

That moment changed everything. It was a turning point rooted in trust—a quiet act of surrender that confirmed what I had long believed: Obedience matters. God pays attention to what we give in silence, to the choices we make when there's no spotlight, no audience, and no applause. That first big yes didn't come in a moment of triumph; it came right at the edge of letting go, when faith had to speak louder than fear. From that day on, I walked with a deeper steadiness. Trust became my business plan, and it outperformed every spreadsheet. I had full confidence in the One writing the story.

When Sysco placed their order, production stretched beyond what I could manage in a single kitchen. I partnered with a bakery to help. Then another. Then two more.

Before long, four bakeries were making my cookies, each adding its own little hum to this growing, wonderfully unlikely operation.

Stores kept ordering. People kept talking about the cookies. Luke and I thought it was all pretty exciting and it felt good to see things finally taking off.

Chapter 8

HAND-MIXED AND HEAVEN-SENT

How Small Beginnings Become Big Miracles

In 2021, during the height of the pandemic, my world of cookies crumbled faster than a stale biscotti. The bakeries I worked with shut down without warning, and suddenly I had more than a thousand cookies stacked in the back of my car, a sugar-loaded ticking time bomb. I had seven days before they all went bad. So I did the only thing that made sense. I joined the Anchorage To Go Facebook group, posted some photos of my cookies, and offered to deliver them right to people's doorsteps. Alaska is no small patch of land, but there I was, driving 45 minutes one way just to drop off cookies.

One delivery changed everything. A woman met me outside her house and asked if I had ever thought about being on QVC. Of course. My mom had been obsessed with QVC. She even managed to rack up $3,000 worth of orders from her nursing home, the operators remembering her like she was family. For me, getting on QVC wasn't just a dream; it was a way to make my mom proud.

That woman gave me a number for her friend Debrah, who had been on QVC herself. Debrah told me to send her cookies first, to prove I was good enough. I sent them, holding my breath. She loved them and connected me to Frank, her QVC guy. Frank was a big deal in the "as seen on TV" universe, a man who had traveled the world to make products happen. I sent him cookies, too, every penny I had going into those boxes, and he called back to say they were good. Really good. The kind of good that could change things. But, he said, I needed production lined up.

I had no idea what that meant. So I did what anyone would do in my situation. I googled "cookie factory." I was half-expecting Willy Wonka to answer the phone. Instead, I found out about co-packers. There was a website called PartnerSlate with hundreds of numbers, and I called them all. The first hundred told me no. The second day I called them all back, they all told me no again. By the third day of rejection, I was practically shouting into the void. Finally, Mark and Ron at Golden Grains in North Carolina agreed to the offer. I think it was more mercy than enthusiasm, but mercy counts.

With that yes, Frank helped me prepare for QVC. By November 2021, it was showtime. Since it was still COVID times, we Skyped from my home. Suddenly, five minutes before we were to go live, everything went haywire. My kitchen lights blew out, the breaker refused to come back on, and I was running around like a wild woman, dragging lamps and Christmas lights as extension cords into place. I propped them up with boxes and Bibles, trying to look professional while my computer battery drained like a melting Popsicle. On top of that, I never got to meet my host before we went live. She talked fast, knowing nothing about me, so I had to jump in and talk over her to tell my story.

Somehow, in eight minutes, I sold $30,000 worth of cookies. It wasn't the sellout I wanted, but it was a start. When the broadcast ended, Frank called right away. "Great job, Molly B," he said. He never calls me Molly, always Molly B. That night, I asked him to be part of my team. I told him I couldn't pay much, but I wanted him with me.

He said yes. He told me I was a disrupter and he loved what I was doing. Five years later, Frank is the vice president of my company and has become like family. That day changed my life forever. I finally believed I had something to be proud of, and others agreed. I had a real brand.

Molly Bz cookies have now been sold in thousands of locations across the nation. In stores like Walmart, 7-Eleven, Costco, Amazon, Target, World Market, and more. They have also been sold in several countries and have been used for the Emmy, Grammy, and Oscar gifting suites, on *Wheel of Fortune*, and even Super Bowl gifting suites. Molly Bz Cookies became a national brand in just three years. This is what the supernatural favor of God in business looks like.

WHEN SMALL-TOWN POWER SAID NO

Success doesn't always knock. Sometimes it rolls up to the drive-through window in a new BMW, five years late, holding a coffee and a quiet smile.

By the time Molly Bz had picked up steam, the taco trailer was long gone, my recipes had grown loud and bold, and I had finally learned how to sell cookies without losing sleep or money. Yes, Molly Bz had become a national brand in just three years. But even then, after the big orders and the jaw-dropping moments of provision, there were places I hadn't revisited. People I hadn't seen. One of those places was a little coffee hut in my hometown. And not just any hut. This one had history.

A few years earlier, when I was broke and barely hanging on, I asked a friend, the owner of that hut, if she would consider carrying my cookies. She said maybe, but her managers would have to approve them first. These women weren't strangers. They had once been regulars at my old bar back when I was running the show. Now the roles had reversed. They had steady jobs and a sliver of local power, and I was the one scraping by. From the way they looked at me, I could tell they liked it that way.

I pulled together what little I had left and made it happen. I used the last of my grocery money to make that first batch. I wrapped each cookie by hand, labeled the flavors, and packed them carefully. Then I dropped them off and waited.

After a couple of days, I called my friend, the owner. She told me the managers decided to pass. They said they didn't like the cookies. I knew that wasn't true. That batch was solid. I always tasted each batch, and those had turned out especially good. But the truth didn't seem to matter. What mattered was that saying no gave them a little boost. They got to turn down Molly from the old days. They got to feel like they were in charge now.

A few weeks later, I got another call. The same managers wanted to try again. This time may be different. So I did it all over again. Another batch. Another 20 bucks. More handwritten labels, four more hours, and more hope packed into a simple box.

After several days of waiting, I drove to the hut myself. One of the managers was working that day. I smiled and asked if they had tried the second batch. She barely looked at me. "Yeah," she said. "It's just not a good fit for us." That was it. No explanation, no feedback. Just a flat "no" served with a smirk.

I said thank you and drove away, heart bruised and stomach hollow. That kind of moment doesn't crush you outright. It just chips away. Not because it defines you, but because it dares you to believe that maybe your story is over.

But it wasn't.

Years passed. The business grew. Life moved forward in ways no one could have predicted. And one day, while visiting my dad, I found myself back in that same little town. The coffee at that hut was actually pretty good, so I pulled in. And there she was. Same young woman, same window, still pouring lattes for the same small-town traffic.

She looked at me as if trying to recall a face from a long time ago. "How's your little cookie business going?" she asked. "Whatever happened to that?"

I didn't flinch. I smiled and said, "You should google me." She blinked. "Wait, what?" I repeated myself. "Just google me. It'll be fun." Then I took my coffee and drove off.

There wasn't a trophy, a headline, or a parade. Just a moment with a strong cup of coffee and a peace that settled deep in my chest. Sometimes grace walks back into the room where rejection once sat. And when it does, you don't need to say much. Just show up, order your coffee, keep going, and thank God for all He has done.

FROM CONSOLATION COOKIES TO CENTER STAGE

And I kept going, entering every angel investment competition in Alaska. All of them. I lugged in my samples, pasted on a smile, and whispered a prayer that this may be the one. But time after time, it was a no. The prize money and press went home with somebody else, while I packed up my folding table, handed out a few leftover cookies like consolation prizes, and drove off empty-handed.

Looking back, I probably gave away hundreds of cookies in those years, currency in a game that never tilted in my favor. Still, I held on to the belief that somewhere, somehow, the right person would eventually say, "I believe in you." And here's the wild twist: Those competitions I never won? My company has outlasted and outgrown most of the winners. Life has a sense of humor that way. Even better, some of those same events have invited me back, not to compete, but to be the keynote speaker. I even get to chip into the prize fund. Talk about full circle.

But not full circle like a victory lap. It feels more like grace, like a reminder that losing doesn't disqualify you. Panels don't get the final say on your purpose. A no is rarely the end of the road. More often, it's God's way of nudging you toward the next turn. Rejection can serve as redirection, protection, or even a blessing.

But that's the thing about noes. Each rejection doesn't just close doors; it clears paths. Sometimes the rejection itself makes room for a stranger, a holier kind of idea to slip in sideways. And in my case, rejection delivered its gift most unexpectedly, while I was asleep.

God slipped me the idea for the Air Fryer Cookie in a

dream, the way a mischievous uncle might slip you a lottery ticket just to see what you'd do with it. I woke up with the packaging already burned into my brain, giant letters shouting "Air Fryer Cookie," as if God Himself had gone into branding. The blueprint arrived fully formed. Par-baked dough waiting for a three-minute fried sauna in the air fryer, tucked neatly inside a resealable bag like a treasure waiting to be unearthed. Too odd, too specific, too divine to ignore. So I set about making it real.

There was a chance to apply for the Most Innovative Product of the Year award at the Sweets & Snacks Expo in 2025. The entry fee was $400, no small chunk of change, but I went for it. I wasn't chasing the trophy. I just wanted my Air Fryer Cookie to sit on that shelf with the giants. To see it displayed next to the likes of Tate's, Nabisco, and Keebler. That was the dream.

I ordered prototype packaging, contacted my co-packer, and asked them to ship bags of the Air Fryer Cookie straight to the Expo. Somewhere between their loading dock and Indianapolis, things went sideways. The bags that arrived were less than half the size they were supposed to be. Instead of holding a dozen cookies, they could barely squeeze in one. I was already in the air, halfway to Indiana, when I got the message.

By the time the plane touched down, my phone was lighting up like a slot machine. The Expo staff hadn't received what they needed. I called from baggage claim, explained the mix-up, and begged for a little mercy. They told me I could still be considered, but only if I submitted a fresh product by morning. Two bags to Room 120 by 8 AM, plus a complete new application before midnight.

With the Air Fryer Cookies out of the running, I asked if I could submit my Bobadoodles instead. Bobadoodles are bite-size shortbread cookies studded with little boba pearls, a playful nod to bubble tea that adds a soft chew to every bite.

They were another God thing. I felt Him nudge me to create bite-size cookies, and about a week later a company approached me with flavored boba pearls that could go right into the oven. I mixed them into what was supposed to be a snickerdoodle dough, but the co-man I hired couldn't get the dough consistency right in their machines. The pearls kept falling out. Their team suggested switching to a shortbread base because it was a much stiffer dough. I hated the idea; I've always thought shortbread cookies were dry and kind of boring. But we went back and forth for months, tweaking and testing and praying we'd land on something worth eating. Eventually, the Bobadoodle was perfected—soft, buttery little bites that melt in your mouth.

So there I was, hunched over my phone while the luggage carousel spun, typing answers as fast as my fingers would move. I finally made it to the hotel around 6:30 AM, shut my eyes for what felt like eight minutes, and then dragged myself back up. I hobbled through a convention center so massive it felt like Disneyland for snack food—Oreo swings, Keebler elves, the whole circus—carrying my samples in the wrong shoes (classic Molly move).

I dropped off the two bags, only to hear, "Actually, we need thirty-two." I turned around, half limping, half running, back to my booth. This body was not designed for sprinting through trade-show carpet, but I hauled a full case of Strawberry Bobadoodles back to judging with two minutes to spare. Then I collapsed onto a couch and cried. It was exhaustion, impostor syndrome, and that nagging whisper that maybe I didn't belong there.

I called Frank. "I don't think we should've come," I told him. "Little Debbie is here. Hostess is here. Even Khloé Kardashian has a popcorn line. What am I doing in this room?"

"Molly B," he said, "of course you're supposed to be there. You're just tired. Go set up your booth. I'll be there soon."

So I pulled myself together and made a video. Raw, puffy-eyed, honest. I talked about what it feels like to show up in a space that feels too big, with shoes that feel too small. Wayne and Cola (Chad's parents), my ex-in-laws who had become investors, arrived to help, and I finally managed to rest.

Then my phone rang again, an Indianapolis number.

"Is this Molly from Molly Bz Cookies? You've been selected as one of the finalists for Most Innovative New Product Award for baked goods."

I burst into tears, slapped on some makeup, and rushed to the ballroom with Frank, Wayne, and Cola. The place was buzzing with hundreds of industry heavyweights, trophies for best popcorn, best chocolate, and best protein bar. Then came baked goods.

The finalists: Keebler, Tate's, Legendary, and me.

And I won.

When I stepped onstage, the woman who handed me my trophy introduced herself. Her name was Sally. A nod from heaven, where my mom now resided. Flashbulbs popped, the crowd roared, and I raised my trophy high, screaming, "YES!" while Frank looked on and said, "See, Molly B? You're supposed to be here."

That day was living proof of what all those noes in

Celebrating Bobadoodles' win at the 2025 Sweets & Snacks Expo.

Alaska had been teaching me. Rejection is God's protection. Every closed door had been shaping me for the one that finally opened. I had asked for a shelf and God gave me a stage.

Winning that trophy was a moment I'll never forget. It lit a fire under everything we were building and gave our team fresh wind in our sails. Momentum, though, doesn't always lead to immediacy. After the confetti settles and the bags are unpacked, there's still a long road of waiting, following up, and holding your breath while the world catches up to the seed God just planted.

So we kept showing up. More emails, more calls, more samples sent out with handwritten notes and fingers crossed. The interest was palpable; you could feel it, but everything moved at the pace of corporate time: slower than you'd like, just fast enough to keep you engaged.

One of those conversations was with Kroger.

We pitched them in June, and they said they'd let us know by the end of the month. July wandered by without a word. Silence, in business, usually means someone politely ghosts you. So we shrugged, filed it under "almost," and turned our focus elsewhere.

Then on July 31, with the month all but packed away, the phone rang. Not only was it a yes, it was a yes to the entire Western region. Not five stores. Not a test market. All of it. No fanfare. No warning. Just a green light where we thought we'd hit drywall.

And that's how I've learned God works. Rarely early, but never late. Always just strange enough to make sure you know it wasn't your doing. What looked like a dead end was just a hallway we hadn't walked far enough down. And

I have learned to praise Him in the hallway until the door opens.

When things fall through, I've learned not to take it personally. It took me years and more than a few bruised feelings, but one story helped me make peace with it. Someone once said you could have the most gorgeous, ripe, sweet peach in the world, and there will still be folks who just don't like peaches.

So, when someone turns down my cookies, I don't crumble. I just figured they're not a peach person, and that's fine. I don't like tomatoes, after all, and that doesn't mean the tomato did anything wrong. Over time, I've come to realize that business, like life, isn't about pleasing every palate. It's about finding the people who are meant to enjoy what you bring to the table.

That's why my brother Andy's diner has shirts that say "We're not trying to please everyone. Just a solid 75 percent." And that's the spirit I try to carry now.

Chapter 9

SWEETER TOGETHER

By most measures, I was finally winning—the kind that shines brightly and refuses to slip by unnoticed. This felt bright and substantial, the kind of success that comes from showing up, staying the course, and refusing to let the hard parts have the final word. The business was thriving, orders were steady, and the chaos that used to run my days had begun to settle into something closer to rhythm. Life no longer felt like a string of emergencies; it was starting to feel like something I had shaped with intention.

There was pride in that. A steady, quiet confidence that had grown from persistence and vision. I had built something meaningful, and for the first time in a long while, I had room to look around and really see it.

But success has a way of drawing attention to what's missing too. In the quiet moments, I began to notice the empty seats. Some were left behind gently, while others were left by silence, distance, or years of unspoken things. While I had been pouring myself into building, certain connections had loosened without my realizing it. And once I saw it, I couldn't unsee it.

This chapter is about people. The ones who stayed through the chaos. The ones who circled back and the restoration that unfolded along the way. For me, that looked like a brother who became a friend, a husband who came home, and a mother whose voice reached me again after years of absence.

And yes, it's about cookies, too, because somehow, in the middle of business meetings, frosting mishaps, and late-night orders, cookies became the bridge. They brought laughter to hard days and reminded me that sweetness still had a place in the story.

Maybe that's what I hope for you. That as you build whatever it is you're building, the work of your hands becomes more than a product. Maybe it becomes a connector, a comfort, or a way through because, sometimes, what we create has the power to carry healing further than we ever imagined.

RING, RING . . . IT'S MOM AGAIN

Some chapters of life don't begin with a thunderclap revelation. Sometimes they start with a phone ringing. Then ringing again. And again. And again.

This was at the very beginning of my cookie life, when I was baking eight to ten hours a day just to keep up—mixing dough, pulling trays, packing orders, praying the business would grow. And right in the middle of all that, my mom started calling. Sometimes she'd ring because she was lonely, sometimes because she was confused, and sometimes because she had slipped out of the assisted living facility again—and I was always the one they called, no matter what I was in the middle of.

At first, I thought I was imagining it. The calls came at random hours—mornings, the lunch rush, sometimes even after midnight. And every time, it was the same familiar voice on the other end asking, "Molly? Can you bring me ice cream?" or "They're stealing my stuff," or "How many cookies did you sell today?"

Eventually, I started counting. Twenty-five times in a day. It turns out my brothers had programmed her phone with speed dial numbers, and Sam, equal parts mischief and affection, had made me number one. One button, and she was calling me, whether I was frosting cookies, in a business meeting, or barely holding it together. She had no idea it was happening so often, and honestly, I never had the heart to stop her. Because with her dementia was something tender and unexpected: my mom's voice, reaching toward me.

I started timing my visits carefully, learning to catch those rare windows when her mind was clear. People with dementia have unpredictable rhythms, and sundowning, those late-afternoon episodes of confusion, are almost a guarantee. Sometimes she was fully herself. Sometimes not. But when the fog lifted, even briefly, it felt like finding treasure.

One day, I walked in and saw it in her eyes. She was there—really there. We laughed about cookies and how she once thought I was crazy for thinking I could sell them. Then her expression changed. She reached for my hand and said, "Molly, I'm so sorry. For all the things I did. You didn't deserve it. I love you. Please forgive me." My heart cracked wide open. The ache I had carried since I was a teenager began to lift. I told her I loved her. I told her I forgave her. And I meant it.

We talked about the Lord, about healing, and about the kind of love that doesn't keep score. After that moment, I wanted to show up for her in ways I never had before. The wackadoodle moments didn't stop. She still accused the staff of stealing, believed the walls were watching her, and for a whole week, no one could figure out why her blood sugar was spiking. Turns out, the freezer was being raided nightly. A review of the security footage showed her scooting down the hall at 1 AM and breaking into the kitchen freezer for ice cream. They eventually had to padlock the door.

When the care facility conducted a food poll, I asked if she wanted to weigh in. I read her the list, hoping she'd reminisce about recipes or offer a restaurant-worthy suggestion. But she had only one answer: "More ice cream." I asked again. Same response. That was her answer, no matter the question.

As unpredictable as things got, there were still sacred flashes of connection. She'd always ask, "How many cookies did you sell today?" Then she'd call my brothers to proudly report, "Molly sold all the cookies in the land." It was silly, but those calls carried healing. Slowly, things inside our family began to shift.

Jay had taken over managing Mom's books alongside his wife, Marta, and with it, he saw the truth of every payment I had made. All the years of confusion and resentment began to unravel. The stories she had told, the ones that shaped how my brothers saw me, started falling apart. Forgiveness didn't arrive in a grand moment; it came in small pieces. Through clarity. Through proximity. Through the quiet courage of seeing things as they were.

Andy and I had a complicated history, marked by years of silence, friction, and distance. But when I stepped in to care for Mom and began managing her house, he picked up the phone. "I just want to thank you for everything you're doing. It's really selfless. And I appreciate it." Then he cried. And told me he loved me. That was the moment everything began to change.

From there, we stayed connected. Our conversations weren't about fixing the past. They were about family, faith, and what mattered now.

ANDY, THE COOKIE COLLABORATOR

Before we ever talked about forgiveness or faith, Andy and I connected through food. He ran restaurants. I baked cookies. And even when other parts of our relationship felt distant or complicated, food was the one thing that never got tangled. It gave us something to dream about, something to create, something to laugh over. I'd be working on a new flavor, and Andy would call with ideas—"You should try this," "What about that?"—like he was moonlighting as my personal cookie consultant. I joked that if he ever sold his restaurant, I'd hire him full-time just to develop flavors. I even sent him a 50-pound bag of cookie flour once so that he could test his ideas in his own kitchen and report back. That's how much we talked about it. But the calls weren't just about cookies.

They were about our kids. Our struggles. We hoped that God was still writing good things for our families. Some nights, we'd pray on the phone—laying it all out for God, no sugarcoating, just the kind of raw honesty that only works when the person on the other end knows what it feels like to carry that kind of love and that kind of worry at the same time.

One of those moments I'll never forget was when Andy's mother-in-law was dying. He called me, voice steady but urgent, and said, "How do I bring her to the Lord?" He wanted her to know Jesus, to be at peace. I pulled over my car and walked him through what to say, how to pray. A few minutes later, he called back. She had been unconscious, but he said the prayer anyway. And then, miraculously, she opened her eyes, whispered, "Thank you," and slipped back into silence. He told me he knew she was at peace. And I knew, in that moment, how far Andy and I had come. That he would call me in that sacred moment was one of the greatest honors of my life.

Andy became more than my brother in those years. He became my mentor, my confidant, my rock. He and his wife, Norann, were steady voices of encouragement, always pointing me back to what really mattered. He didn't just give advice. He asked for it too. And that meant something. So did the way he showed up, again and again, as my cheerleader. We shared pictures of our grandbabies. We teased each other like kids. We texted all the time. And whenever something good happened, Andy would call and say something I hadn't heard a lot growing up: "*I'm proud of you.*"

He meant it. And I needed it.

Andy was 15 years older than me, but he never made me feel small. He was strong, loyal, protective, and kind. The kind of man who had no enemies unless you messed with his family or his business. Then you'd better brace yourself. He didn't hold grudges, but he didn't tolerate harm either. He carried conviction and kindness in equal measure. He reminded me to stop trying to please people who were never going to approve. To stop carrying weight

I wasn't meant to take. He knew the voices I was still battling in my head because he'd grown up with them too. Sam and I reconnected during that time, too, and by God's grace, every relationship in our family that had once been strained was somehow made whole.

AARON AND THE LONG WAY BACK

By the time the divorce was finalized, Aaron and I had already been living apart in every way that mattered. The signatures, the court filings, and the untangling of shared space were just the final punctuation on a sentence that had been slowly losing its voice. We no longer shared a home, a rhythm, or a vision. What we once promised each other had faded into silence, and yet, somewhere deep in me, the echo of that covenant remained. We had a son together. A history. A belief I couldn't shake that when God joins two lives, He doesn't treat that lightly.

This wasn't about holding on to the past. I wasn't waiting in the shadows, hoping he'd walk back through the door. Life kept moving, and so did I. I raised Luke with all the steadiness I had. I built a business from the ground up and laughed again, even when my heart still carried bruises. I stitched myself back together with bakery string, whispered prayers, and the kind of stubborn hope that doesn't require a guarantee. Through all of it, I kept praying, not for a return, but for redemption that Aaron would encounter God in a way that softened whatever had hardened inside him. I wanted peace for him. Wholeness. A future that didn't feel so fractured. And in the hidden corners of my heart, I held on to the quiet hope that maybe, just maybe, that kind of healing might lead him back to us.

There was one prayer I returned to again and again, words lifted from Scripture and etched into my daily routine like breath itself: "God, turn his heart of stone into a heart of flesh." I whispered it while pouring coffee, spoke it aloud in the car after school drop-off, and carried it into the stillness before sleep. I didn't need to see change overnight. I simply needed to believe that something unseen was beginning to shift, even if the ground still looked hard and dry.

When I found out he was dating someone else, a woman I had once called a friend, the ache was sharp but unsurprising. She had blocked me from every corner of her digital life, and the silence between us said everything words never could. It hurt. Of course it did. But I didn't interfere.

I didn't chase. I didn't argue with a reality I couldn't control. I just kept praying, trusting that God could move in places I couldn't reach.

Eventually, word came that they'd broken up. I sat with that news for a few days, letting it settle, allowing it to stir. On an ordinary afternoon with nothing remarkable in the air, I sent Aaron a message. It wasn't emotional or loaded; it was light, a small flirtation, the kind of easy banter that carried the memory of what we used to share. He responded with warmth. Something opened. We began talking again, tentatively at first. It felt like walking into a familiar room that had been rearranged, recognizable, but different enough that we both moved slowly, careful not to trip over what used to be.

We started dating again. Hesitantly. Hopefully. With a mixture of affection and fear. The feelings were real, but the past lingered at the edges, reminding us of what had once gone wrong. We took small steps forward, then pulled back when it felt too tender. But we didn't walk away. We kept showing up, uncertain but willing.

Not long after, he accepted a job in Eagle River, 20 minutes from Anchorage. I hadn't said anything about relocating, but when he told me he took the job because he figured I'd end up there eventually, something in me paused. At the time, I was still in Soldotna—balancing school pick-ups, karate classes, and long bakery nights that came with running a growing business. Anchorage felt like another world. But sometimes, God starts preparing the next chapter long before you realize you're being moved.

Aaron began visiting on weekends to spend time with Luke. When he stayed, he slept at the house. After Luke was tucked in and the dishwasher hummed in the background, we'd sit on the couch, side by side, letting the quiet wrap around us. We didn't define what was happening. We didn't need to. The space between us had shifted. The intensity we once knew had softened into something steadier, less like wildfire and more like a slow-burning flame.

Eventually, I moved to Eagle River. When I did, we found a place with three bedrooms. A setup that gave us space and structure while we figured out what this new version of us could be. We slept in separate rooms, lived in separate rhythms under the same roof, but the connection was there, clear and growing. We hadn't spoken the words yet, but we both knew we were in it again.

During that season, I continued praying. Sometimes, I'd dab a little anointing oil on his pillow or on the soles of his shoes. It wasn't a ceremony or a secret plea. It was simply a quiet invitation for God to fill the atmosphere, for His presence to guide the parts of Aaron that still felt unsure.

At some point, I invited him to church. Ours is a place full of life and expectancy. The worship is unfiltered and alive, hands raised, voices unrestrained, people clapping, singing, and meeting God in powerful, visible ways. I had been healed at church myself, my failing eyesight restored during prayer I'll never forget. I had seen others rise from wheelchairs, bodies and hearts mended before my eyes. For Aaron, it was unlike anything he'd ever known. Loud. Unfamiliar. Raw. But he kept coming. Sunday after Sunday, he stood beside me, still figuring out what he believed, but willing to show up. That meant more to me than any declaration ever could.

At the time, he was splitting his nights between our house and his parents' home while waiting for his own place to be finished. We didn't rush the conversation. We just lived with the questions, allowing space for clarity to rise when it was ready. And slowly, it did.

Then came the Oscars.

The cookie business had opened an unexpected door that led me to Los Angeles for a special event for the Oscars gifting suites. I asked Aaron if he would stay with Luke while I was gone, and he agreed without a moment of hesitation.

When I returned, he was standing in the kitchen, grounded and open, carrying a kind of peace I hadn't seen in him for years.

"I miss you," he said quietly. "I love you. I love Luke. I even love cookies. And I don't know why I keep pushing away the one thing that feels like home."

I smiled and said, "Then stop."

But I followed it with what had always been at the center of my heart. "I love you," I told him, "but I can't move forward unless you give your heart to the Lord."

Aaron had always been a man who valued truth. If he were going to surrender his life, it wouldn't be for show. He needed to believe it, deeply, entirely, for himself. And three weeks later, he did. He walked to the front of the church with quiet conviction and opened his life to God.

Two months after that, we were married again.

But this time, we didn't return to what once was. We stepped into something new. A fresh foundation. A deeper partnership. We pray together now, over our home, our children and grandchildren, our work, and each other. I no longer drink. He rarely does. We talk more, we forgive faster, and the things that once pulled us apart have no place in this chapter.

Luke is thriving, growing into the kind of young man I

always prayed he would be. Emerald moved to Washington and now works as my marketing manager. She married an amazing young man—also named Aaron—and together they made us grandparents to a sweet little boy, Henry Norman, and a little girl on the way. Anni moved back to Alaska to be closer to family, and she's constantly sparking fresh ideas for Molly Bz that keep us dreaming bigger. We've come a long way, and I don't take a single step of it for granted.

This year, Aaron and I celebrated our four-year anniversary. I still look at him the way I did when we first fell in love, with soft eyes, a full heart, and a grateful spirit. And I plan to grow old beside him. Because when God restores something, He doesn't hand back a shattered version. He makes it new. He makes it whole.

FAITH IS THE SECRET INGREDIENT

The timeline isn't neat, and the memories don't fall into tidy order. They surface the way life usually does—one moment blending into another until only the turning points stay sharp. One of those was New York. My first Fancy Food Show. The city buzzed like it was lit from underneath, and I moved through it on pure electricity. Frank—who'd once been a stranger and now knew every shortcut, deli, and bagel cart—guided me and my assistant Kayla through it all like we were part of some beloved local ritual.

We were there to launch Bobadoodles for the very first time, a July 2023 show when those little boba-studded shortbread bites finally stepped into the spotlight. I thought we'd pick up a few accounts, maybe gather a couple stories to take home. Instead, it lit a fuse. Buyers tasted them, smiled, and started talking. That spark set off a ripple that reached farther than I expected.

Five Below called. Then World Market. And around that same stretch of time, Walmart invited us to their Open Call in 2023. Fourteen thousand people applied, only 700 were given in-person meetings, and we were one of them. Frank and I flew to Bentonville with two pitches on the schedule and one hope in our minds: a golden ticket. I arrived with a terrible flu and could hardly stand, so I prayed for a small window of strength. Within five minutes in the shower the fever lifted and my body felt clear. I met Frank in the hotel lobby and he smiled and said, "Let's go get our golden ticket." We walked out with two. Only three brands received two golden tickets that year, and Molly Bz was one of them. We were approved for both Grab and Go and the cookie and cracker aisle. After the meetings, I spent a week recovering at my brother's home in the Bentonville area, already thinking about what this new chapter with Walmart would become.

By then, Frank had become my partner in crime, not by title, not at first, but by presence. He was the one who sat next to me in the chaos after QVC, who kept pace through the Oscars, who navigated SnackMagic and Great Wolf

Me and Frank visiting World Market headquarters.

Lodge and every expo that followed. When we started, I could barely pay him. I offered what I could, first a little, then enough to count. Now, as vice president, he comes to every show, runs the day-to-day, and when people ask how we make it work, he just shrugs and says, "Molly, it's you and me to the end."

Just a few days before Christmas 2024, I got the call no sister ever wants to receive. It was 4 AM when the phone rang. On the other end was Norann, Andy's wife, my sister-in-law, and someone who had become a dear friend. Her voice was trembling as she told me Andy had been found on the kitchen floor in the middle of the night. I reached for a pen, expecting to write down a hospital name and room number. But then she said the words that stopped everything: He was gone. A heart attack. The kind they call the widow-maker.

When my brother Andy died, I told Frank he'd have to fill those shoes, in the business and in my life. He wasn't born my brother, yet he became one.

He's not the only one who stepped in or stepped up. Kayla, who once worked as my assistant and traveled with me to expos and events, was there in the early, scrappy days. She packed cookies, hauled boxes, and helped me figure it out as we went. Life eventually shifted her toward motherhood and teaching, but she still holds a special place in my story. She was more than an assistant, more like a co-dreamer during those first big leaps.

Brianna, my niece, started doing my content before she had any formal training. Now she's in high demand, because talent finds its way when someone believes in it. Sam, my only full-blood brother, who used to fight me like it was his job, is now one of my greatest supporters. He's the one coming with me to Vegas, along with Wayne and Cola.

There's Jay, my brother, one of the best men I have ever met, who never drank, never drifted, worked hard, and always loved steadily and quietly. His wife, Marta—the dessert queen and a cancer survivor—is a walking miracle. There's Tony, whose joy and talent fill every room, and Jackie, solid beside him. Sean, the cook and musician, tells stories and jokes no one else could invent. Jesse, who's been my brother since he was two, has always carried more weight than he lets on. He's a hardworking, fun family man. Christi, my sister from another mister, wears her faith like armor and raises her four children with strength and laughter. And Luci, Skip's daughter, became my biggest investor and one of my closest friends. She believed in me with more than just words. She put her money behind it—and her heart too.

But not everyone is still here. We've known loss. My brother Leland died in a motorcycle accident, and Jason from cancer. The kind of grief that rearranges you from the inside out. But love didn't leave when they did. It stayed. It stretched. It made room for more.

My dad, Norm, Mr. Rock Steady, is still anchoring all of us at nearly 80. His wife, Barbara, who cooks like heaven, lives in her kitchen and gives grace to anyone who enters her home. Andy and I used to agree she is the best cook around, besides us. He would have loved knowing that Emerald's little boy carries Dad's name.

There's no way to name everyone who showed up when I needed them most, because the list would stretch too far to hold. Some came with prayers whispered faithfully, others with generosity that met practical needs, and still others with the simple gift of presence, staying when it would have been easier to walk away. In their own ways, each one reminded me of the same truth—that God is steady, unfailing, and faithful, and that He never wastes people or pain.

I still keep that scripture close—the one my mom wrote out years ago and I later found, folded near my foot. Proverbs 16:3: Commit your actions to the Lord and your plans will succeed.

The business kept growing, and with it the table seemed

to expand, making room for more people to pull up chairs, for more hands to join the work, and for more prayers to be spoken over what we had become. I had thought I was simply building a company, measuring progress in orders and accounts, but what God was really giving me was a way back to the people I loved, a way to restore what had once felt fractured. In the end, I didn't only discover success; I discovered family again, and with them beside me, I knew I was finally home.

Chapter 10

THE KIND OF MAGIC YOU CAN TASTE

It's strange, looking back, how something so simple could grow into something so big. I didn't plan any of this. I just kept saying yes—to the work, the risk, and the next right thing. Somehow, that was enough.

If you had told me years ago that my cookies would one day end up at the Emmys, the Oscars, and the Grammys, I would've believed you. Maybe not in the timing, but in the promise. I always knew these cookies had a story to tell—I just didn't know how far it would travel. Molly Bz went from being mixed by hand in a little Alaskan kitchen to showing up in the gifting suites for some of the biggest shows in the world. Every time I see one of those moments come full circle, I can't help but shake my head and smile.

The journey's been surreal. From meeting incredible people at those events who genuinely love the brand to watching *Wheel of Fortune* give away "Molly Bz cookies and milk for a year," and hearing Pat Sajak say my company's name out loud on national TV, it's been one incredible "How did I get here?" after another.

But behind every headline moment is the same heartbeat that started this all: curiosity, prayer, and a wooden spoon. Every flavor I've ever created began with a little research and a lot of faith. I've made it a habit to look up the top 10 food trends each year because by the time most people catch on, I've already been experimenting in the kitchen. That's how the Hot Cheeto cookie happened. I saw that spicy snacks were trending and thought, why not put it in a cookie? The same thing happened with Earl Grey Lavender Lemon. Those flavors were everywhere in 2019, so I figured it was time they met some butter and sugar.

Following the trends led to one of the most incredible surprises of all. In 2024, I got an email from Food Network. They wanted to include Molly Bz Bobadoodles in their "2024 Food Trends to Watch." I'd spent years researching trends, chasing them, adapting to them, and suddenly, I was one. That moment stopped me in my tracks. I went from googling the trends to being the trend. It still gives me chills when I think about it.

Those were pinch-me moments, no doubt. But the truth is, I never saw them as accidents. They were divine reminders that the work wasn't in vain, that the same God who opened doors I never could have knocked on myself was still guiding every step.

The more the brand grew, the more I understood that success isn't about how far you go, but who goes with you. Every open door became proof that God works through people who care enough to keep walking beside you. And if there's one thing I've learned, it's that He never meant for us to build anything alone.

BUILDING SOMETHING BIGGER

The wild thing about growth is that it doesn't always look like expansion. Sometimes it looks like trust. It looks like handing off a piece of your dream and realizing it's safer in someone else's hands than you expected. That's been the real story of Molly Bz. The shelves and store launches are exciting, but the miracle has always been the people who showed up along the way.

Frank has been my constant. He's the calm in the middle of my chaos, the one who reminds me that we've figured out every hard thing before, so why would this be any different? Emily brings order to my whirlwind. She's quick, precise, and joyful, like a metronome that keeps the beat steady while the rest of us play a little off-tempo. Frank and I always say we should make hats that read TGFE—Thank God For Emily—because it's true every single day.

My daughter Emerald keeps the brand alive with her creativity and spark. She has this beautiful way of translating heart into marketing. Brianna, my niece, has that same gift. Her photos somehow capture the soul of what we do. They're full of color, joy, and a little sweet rebellion. When I see her work, I think to myself, this is what love looks like when it learns to bake. And then there's Anni, my daughter who is our idea gal. She dreams up the super fun concepts, like the Naughty and Nice campaign now in Target stores—that one was all her. She also jumps in on graphic design projects, working under Emerald's direction. Emily oversees Emerald and Brianna, and I oversee Emily. It keeps everything running smoothly, without letting family blur the lines of business.

I still create all the flavors and ideas, the same way I did in my kitchen during those early days. Once I perfect a recipe, that's when the real work begins. It gets handed off to the co-packers, where it becomes a formula. From there, the nutrition labels are made, the packaging is designed, the boxes or pouches are selected, and the case packs, pallet configurations, and weights are all determined. Sometimes one store will need 29 different trucks, and coordinating all of that is its own job—Frank handles the logistics of where the cookies are picked up and where they're headed. I work with eight co-man partners at this stage of the journey, each with their own strengths. Some max out at nine pallets, while others won't even start unless we're running fifty. They all have a place, and together we make this thing work. Bonnie Boo Boo, Rick, and Bob in Washington help with recipe development and scaling my experiments for full production. Suzy and Franz, the young couple in Detroit, handle our Target runs with so much heart and hustle. Patrick and Sophie in New York are our newest partners, full of energy and support from day one. Watching each of them grow brings me back to the early days—full of fear, fire, and faith that somehow it would all come together.

Even our partners have become part of the family. Brian Duffy, a mentor who became family, Nathan with his sharp mind for numbers, and Daniel, the cookie lawyer who's been there from the very beginning, all play their part in this beautiful mix. What we have is more than business. It's laughter on conference calls and prayers before big decisions. It's a team built on kindness, purpose, and belief.

This is what happens when you stop trying to build an empire and start building something eternal. Something baked with love, seasoned with prayer, and wrapped in joy. That's what makes it rise.

Every package still carries Genesis 50:20: *What Satan meant for evil, God will use for good.* It is not decoration. It is the story printed on my bones. I walked out of that season with more than a business. I walked out with peace that made no sense, joy that surfaced even in exhaustion, and a faith that steadied me when everything else wobbled.

All big things start small. Mine began in a food trailer on the side of the road that smelled of halibut and hope. When people ask how I did it, I do not hand out formulas. I tell them the truth: I did not quit. I trusted God. And He made a way where there had only been a gravel shoulder, a borrowed fryer, and the wild idea that this story was not finished yet.

COMING HOME

I still remember being that girl in Alaska, watching my parents hustle through one business after another and learning that work and faith often had to walk hand in hand. Back then, I dreamed of doing something that mattered, even when I had no idea what it would be. I just knew I wanted to create something that brought joy and connection. I could never have imagined it would one day lead me here.

Of all the incredible things that have happened with the company, from being featured by Food Network to partnerships with major retailers, the one that means the most to me is this: We finally came home to Alaska.

For years, production had outgrown what Alaska could handle, so everything happened in the Lower 48. I hadn't sold a single cookie in my home state for ages. But now that is changing. A new distributor brought Molly Bz products into stores across Alaska starting in January 2026, and it feels like everything has come full circle.

When the first Target in Alaska sold out of nearly 200 cookies in 10 days, I could not stop smiling. That moment wasn't just about sales. It was about showing my dad what this dream had become and letting him see the fruit of all those years of hard work, prayers, and second chances.

My dad, Norm, is the kind of man who never wavers. He has worked hard his entire life, cared deeply for our family, and taught me what it means to stand firm when life gets messy. He is one of the good ones, steady and loyal, the kind of man who holds the center when everything else feels uncertain. Watching him light up when local Channel 2 News ran a story about Molly Bz was priceless. He might not fully understand what it means to be a national brand, but when the shelves across Alaska are stocked with our cookies, he will see it. And I cannot wait for that.

I am so grateful that my stepmom, Barbara, has been right there too. She is warm, grounded, and full of grace. Together, they have been anchors for our family, steady through every season.

Coming home feels different this time. Not as a comeback, but as a promise kept. It feels like God is letting me walk back into the place where it all began, only this time I am carrying proof of what faith can do. Alaska raised me. It taught me to work hard, to trust big, and to believe that, even from the smallest snow-covered town, God can bake something beautiful out of your life. Coming home reminded me that the story was never just about where I started. It was about what God could do through the smallest beginnings.

MORE THAN COOKIES

People like to say, "It's just cookies." But I've never believed that for a second. The cookies have always been the vessel, not the destination. They're my little sugary missionaries, carrying joy and conversation wherever they go. Flour and sugar are just the disguise; what they really deliver is hope.

Every place I've traveled has felt like a divine breadcrumb trail. From the bright lights of Los Angeles to the humid air of Florida, the roar of Vegas, the bustle of New York, and the quiet hum of Texas nights, I've prayed over them all. Airports, hotel rooms, loading docks, trade shows—each one a small altar. I don't always know why I'm sent somewhere, but I've learned not to question the route. God draws strange maps, and somehow every line leads back to purpose.

At the World Food Championships, in a crowd of

hundreds, I met a young man named Dan. We started talking about faith right there between the cookie samples and the stage lights. I prayed with him to receive the Lord while his mom listened on speakerphone, tears in her voice. She had been praying for him for years. I'll never forget it. That was the moment I knew again what I've always known. It was never just about cookies. God was simply using them to open hearts.

That's how He works. Subtle, steady, and often hidden inside the ordinary. Every opportunity, every store shelf, and every open door is a divine appointment. My only job is to keep showing up, do the work with excellence, and leave room for God to surprise me.

When I started Molly Bz, I thought maybe it would grow into a national brand. But God had a bigger recipe in mind. Now, with global partnerships and licensing deals, it has become something I could have never mixed up on my own. What thrills me most isn't how far it's reached, but how deep it goes. It reaches into hearts that need to be reminded it's never too late.

I was 45 when I began again. Most people think you're supposed to have it all figured out by 30, but purpose doesn't follow deadlines. Mary Kay was in her mid-40s when she started. Colonel Sanders was 62. You are never too late for the story God is still writing.

My dream now is to create an academy for kids and single moms, the kind of people who just need one yes to change everything. I've been that mom, praying over bills and borrowed time, and I know what a simple act of belief can do. I want to hand that same belief forward.

When the time comes to sell Molly Bz, which I've planned for 2027, I'll pour myself into that next chapter. I want to speak, teach, and help people rebuild their lives. I want to show them that faith and grit make a powerful batter, one that rises even when life forgets to preheat the oven.

Because, in the end, it was never about the cookies. It was about the calling. About saying yes to a God who knows how to turn crumbs into feasts and failures into testimonies. Every bag, every flavor, and every miracle has been proof that He is still in the business of redemption and that He doesn't waste a single grain of sugar.

ACKNOWLEDGMENTS

If you're holding this book, I don't think it's by accident. Books have a funny way of finding people at just the right time. Maybe you were looking for something else, a sign or a spark or a reason to believe that all this mess might still turn into something beautiful. Well, here it is.

I've lived through the kind of chapters that make you wonder if the author fell asleep at the pen. I've had $35 in my bank account and a head full of wild dreams that made no sense to anyone but God. I've faced stacks of bills that looked taller than my faith and watched everything crumble, only to find grace in the rubble. Somewhere between the burnt batches and the answered prayers, I learned that God's timing doesn't run late. It simply runs deep.

If there is one truth I know for sure, it is this: Nothing is wasted. Not the losses, not the detours, not even the long nights when you feel forgotten. Every moment is part of the recipe. Sometimes you think you are just scraping the bowl clean, but really, He is mixing in the miracle.

To my family—my husband, Aaron; my kids, Emerald, Anni, and Luke; my son-in-law, Aaron; and my sweet grandson, Henry—thank you for standing in the kitchen of chaos with me and somehow coming out baked goods. You are the joy that kept me stirring when everything else went quiet.

To my mom, thank you for the grace that came full circle.

To my dad, Norm, and my stepmom, Barbara, thank you for being steady in a world that rarely sits still.

To my brothers Tony, Jay, Sam, Sean, and Jesse, and to Andy, Leland, and Jason, who went home early, thank you for giving me noise and grit and humor and a sense of belonging that carried me farther than you will ever know.

To the friends who became family, the ones who prayed, invested, worked beside me, or simply held me together when life felt heavier than I could explain, your fingerprints are all over this book. I could not name you all without turning these pages into a phone book, but your love is baked into every line.

If you take one thing from these pages, let it be this: All you have to do is try. Do a little digging. Make the call. Say the prayer. Stir the bowl. You never know which small act will be the one that changes everything.

Because the God who met me at rock bottom, when I had $150 to my name and a whole lot of faith holding me up, is the same God who can turn your scraps into a feast. He is still in the business of miracles. He is still using small-town girls, late bloomers, and holy messes to change the world one bite at a time.

And if He can do it for me, the woman who had to start over more than once, He can do it for you too.

ABOUT THE AUTHOR

Molly Blakeley grew up in Alaska, where childhood came with homemade sourdough, midnight sun, and more family businesses than most towns have stoplights. She learned early how to run a register, flip a customer's mood, and build a new idea out of whatever tools and scraps were on hand. By the time she was a teenager, she had already been a bowling instructor, an arcade shark, and a fashion entrepreneur.

As she got older, life opened the door to a whole new parade of ventures and plot twists. Molly has owned and managed floral shops, roller rinks, food carts, bars, a dinner theater, and, briefly, a chicken-scented gift basket shop. She has fallen in love, started over, raised three kids, rebuilt after heartbreak, survived a few turns that would break most people, and somehow turned her last $150 into a taco truck that accidentally birthed a national cookie brand.

Today she is the founder and Chief Mischief Maker of Molly Bz, the company known for cookies so over the top they really should come with a warning label. Her life is a blend of imagination, faith, determination, and the steady instinct to turn unexpected moments into something meaningful, all baked together into stories she has finally decided to share out loud.

Molly still lives in Alaska, where she continues to dream big, pray boldly, laugh loudly, and build things that probably should not work but somehow always do.